B
BACA

Baca, Jimmy
Santiago.

73504

Working in the dark.

$19.95

DATE		

WORKING IN
THE DARK

WORKING IN THE DARK

Reflections of a Poet of the Barrio

Jimmy Santiago Baca

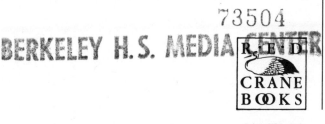

RED CRANE BOOKS

SANTA FE

1995

First Edition

Manufactured in the United States of America

Cover and text design by Paulette Livers Lambert

Cover painting and text drawings by Adan Hernandez

Library of Congress Cataloging-in-Publication Data
Baca, Jimmy Santiago, 1952-
 Working in the dark / Jimmy Santiago Baca. — 1st ed.
  p. cm.
 ISBN 1-878610-08-2
 1. Baca, Jimmy Santiago, 1952- —Biography. 2. Mexican Americans—Social life and customs. 3. Poets, American—20th century—Biography. I. Title
PS3552.A254Z477 1991
811'.54—dc20   91-60328
                                                  CIP

Red Crane Books
826 Camino de Monte Rey
Santa Fe, New Mexico 87501

Contents

Acknowledgments

I wish to thank those who encouraged this book. First, not enough can be said of my two sons, whose insight and compassion gave sustenance to my dance over the burning coals of creativity. Thanks to my *primo*, Gilbert Chavez de Pico Rivera, for his *chingón carnalismo*; and to my *primo, el masiso* Victor Padilla of Brewtown, Burque*: I pray he continues to believe in his healing vision, from which I drew help. This book was born on our ceremonial walks along the Río Grande, under the sun, beside the healing waters of Aztlán in the South Valley.

Pa' los vatos de Sacra y el macheen masiso veterano de St. Anthony's, Rudy Carrillo *y su carnal, el poeta-curandero indígena* José Montoya, for singing the freedom song of our Chicano dream that keeps us believing in our beauty and strengthens our passage into the future. A salute to George Evans and Gary Soto in San Francisco, strong poets whose hearts and hospitality fuse poetry into daily life. Blessings to the spirit of Miguel Piñero, playwright and poet of the highest caliber, a friend I still mourn, whose generous heart was a garden of jeweled roses. I thank Edward Tise and Mojo for their defense of language and their love and understanding of its internal rhythm. My gratitude to Mark Whitney for his dedication to breaking down the borders between races and his outrage at injustice, and Will Inman who continues to speak out bravely and to act against stupidities that deny human beings their dignity.

I want to thank Adrian Louis, from Pine Ridge, for honoring me with a gift of strong spirit-medicine at a critical time in my life. And thanks to those very wonderful brothers from San Anto', José Jiménez and Dr. Roberto Jiménez and

---

*Slang for Albuquerque, N.M.

also his wife Darlene, whose kindness guided me through some of my worst times. Thanks also to James Cobb, with his whiskey runner's gumption and cosmic genius, a gifted painter whose ideas propelled me out to the edge to touch the smoldering tip of God's tongue.

Warm thanks go to Taylor Hackford, director of my film, *Blood In . . . Blood Out* (working title), who rode the exhaustive journey out to its end with humor and integrity and made it a delightful adventure of discovery. Thanks to Bruno Rubeo *y* Mayes for their tremendous hospitality and friendship during the filming of the movie. My appreciation goes also to Gina Blumenfeld, Missy Kelly, and Katherine Moore of the film production company, Vato De Atole Productions, who were there to help me when I was at my wit's end. They were the calm center in my typhoon metamorphosis.

I want to thank Barbara Heizer, for first offering to publish an essay; and Tino Villanueva of Boston, for his generosity in reading through the manuscript and helping to compile the glossary.

My appreciation to Adan Hernandez, *un vato firme y de áquellas*, for his wonderful drawings and his painting on the book jacket. His work is *pura salsa*, life's fire, a rainbow over the land of Aztlán. *Héchale carnal, déjate cael la greña vato . . . es un pinto masiso . . . un carnal de mi cora. Ponle.* Thank you, *carnal*.

I wish to thank Harriet Slavitz for giving her meticulous attention to these essays. Her editorial expertise clarified the ideas where they were murky and strengthened the phonic aspects of the prose where they were flat. Her sustaining belief in the essays, her unwavering faith in the work and her endless editorial support balanced and gave control to the book. I feel fortunate to have her as my editor and friend.

My thanks go also to those many others who keep the sacred fire going and tend the flames, who beat the red drums of their hearts in strong praise of living, and carry on the struggle for dignity and spirituality, without whom this book could not have come to birth. *Gracias.*

Editor's Introduction

Every poet of authentic vocation is a hero, a risk-taker. In search of himself and of hidden verities, he undertakes on our behalf perilous quests through the depths and vertiginous heights of the psychic landscape, a terra incognita miles past the comfortable suburbs most of us inhabit. The illuminations he finds there, and brings back and shapes for us, renovate human experience as no other formulations, no systems of thought (excluding, as they must, some of the fertile chaos of life), can do. The writer, the poet, is both miner and lapidary, delving the mysteries embedded in the disregarded and unworked matter of daily life, carving their hidden facets so that we see them for the first time, or as never before: inspiring us, if we will, to journeys of perception beyond our own familiar boundaries.

Sensitive to the hazards of this task, in which more than a few have foundered—the possibility of derangement from which there is no return—some writers, such as Flaubert, elect lives of bland monotony, of strict outer orderliness as counterbalance and defense against the inner wilderness of their explorations. For others, however, there may not be the luxury of choice. But choice they do make, and one of notable courage. Engaging what has been given, apparently irredeemable circumstances of insecurity and deprivation, in this darkness they seek their vision and find their art. Jimmy Baca may be counted in this company.

Baca's history would seem to be a recipe for disaster. Born into a troubled and impoverished Chicano family at a time, before the politicization of ethnic groups, when anti-Hispanic prejudice was rampant, he was deprived of parental presence in earliest childhood. He then lived with loving grandparents for no more than a year or two before his grandmother's progressive blindness compelled her to send him to an orphange, where, as readers of this book will learn, he received less than tender care. By the age of ten he had run away and was on the streets in the country and city barrios of New Mexico, exposed to the sordidness and hard-pressed vitality that flourish in ghettos everywhere. Alone in a world that offered him meager opportunity to develop and grow, to make something of his life, he wandered aimlessly, eventually taking refuge in alcohol and drugs. A series of imprisonments for minor offenses almost inevitably followed.

There is a tradition of prison literature of which the medieval poet François Villon is one of the most distinguished exponents; among the most gifted in our own time is the playwright Jean Gênet. Villon had the inestimable advantage, for a poet, of a classical education, through his early adoption by a canon of the church. And on the evidence of Gênet's non-dramatic writings we know that prison became the heaven of his desire for a man of his psychosexual proclivities.

For Jimmy Baca there was neither the sustaining cultural resources of a Villon nor the voluptuous acquiescence of a Gênet to buttress him against the brutalities of prison life. His few years of schooling, embittered by racial prejudice and bloody schoolyard brawls, had left him virtually illiterate; and he paid a hard price, the harrowing record of which is recounted in these pages, for persistent defiance and rebellion against the degrading treatment to which he and his fellow prisoners were routinely subjected.

Nevertheless, it was during one of his periods of imprisonment, in a desolate time when it seemed as if everything of human dignity and aspiration had been stripped from him, that he turned to the empowerment of the word. Painfully teaching himself to read and write from a book stolen from one of his warders, Baca entered into his poet's vocation. His eloquent telling of this call, heard and answered in desperation, comprises one of this book's most moving essays.

His readers will not be left in doubt of the accuracy of

Denise Levertov's observation, in her introduction to one of his collections of poetry,* that Baca "writes with unconcealed passion: detachment is not a quality he cultivates." In some respects, the power of his feeling may be more evident in his prose here, in which the sources of his poetry in the sufferings and hard-found celebrations of his life come to us raw. Raw also, but only for prudish readers, may seem some aspects of his language, those pungent words which alone can genuinely reflect the harshness of life in the low taverns and crack alleys of our inner cities, and behind the bars of our 'institutions of correction' (a designation the irony of which Baca tackles head-on here). Those who may take offense are well answered by W.H. Auden's remark that "in literature vulgarity is preferable to nullity, just as grocer's port is preferable to distilled water." Who tastes these essays will not mistake what full-bodied drink is on offer.

But Baca's particular strength is that, both in his poems and in these essays, he moves through and beyond the rough candor with which he gives voice to the personal and inherited rage and pain of the dispossessed. The instruments of his deliverance from a potentially fatal bitterness were two, both attended by conscious commitment: the recovery of cultural traditions, which he follows back to their most ancient roots; and the embracing, with unwavering fidelity, of his poet's gift.

A not uncommon strategy of defense among members of oppressed peoples and minorities is emulation of the oppressor—assimilation; and Baca with typical frankness tells of his own temptations "to be[come] as blue-eyed and blond-haired an American as anyone," because "the pain of being different was too great." But calamity, and his innate honesty, saved him from self-betrayal. Confined to a cellblock with other Chicanos, he was reawakened to the preciousness of his Indian and Hispanic heritages, and made a vow of conscience, since proved with signal constancy, to carry the

---

*Martín & Meditations on the South Valley (New York: New Directions, 1987).

stories of his people to the world. Some of those stories, *canciones* of pride and travail, may be found in these essays, as in many of his poems.

"They sent me to prison for drug possession," Baca tells us here. "And there, out of suffering, I found a reprieve from chaos, found language, and it led me back to the teachings and conduct of my elders. I discovered a reason for living, for breathing, and I could love myself again, trust myself again, trust what my heart dreamed and find the strength to pursue those dreams. . . . In language I have burned my old selves and improvised myself into a new being." In Baca's verse and prose improvisations, sensuous, lyrical, and irrigated with a fundamentally universal wisdom, he leads us through the canyons and *arroyos* of arid lands—his native New Mexico; the earlier years of his life—to the sources of self-discovery in deep waters of the unconscious and of renewal in the mythic place of origin.

And when he rejoices in "the delight[s] of being here!," we must ask ourselves: how does a man survive unstained, with so tender a heart and so innocent an eye, the experiences he has made us privy to? How did he so unerringly find his way through the dark to the pathways of joy?

Hear Jimmy Baca ask and answer such questions, as he best can, in an essay here: "Where does my poetry come from? I answer that I come from poetry, I bear myself on poetry, I walk upright on two feet because of poetry." And again: "What is that spark, where does it come from? Who knows? Only let us celebrate that creation, for this is a mystery we will never understand."

A rare reward awaits the reader who accepts this invitation.

Harriet Slavitz

I
Lock and Key

Coming into Language

On weekend graveyard shifts at St. Joseph's Hospital I worked the emergency room, mopping up pools of blood and carting plastic bags stuffed with arms, legs, and hands to the outdoor incinerator. I enjoyed the quiet, away from the screams of shotgunned, knifed, and mangled kids writhing on gurneys outside the operating rooms. Ambulance sirens shrieked and squad car lights reddened the cool nights, flashing against the hospital walls: gray—red, gray—red. On slow nights I would lock the door of the administration office, search the reference library for a book on female anatomy and, with my feet propped on the desk, leaf through the illustrations, smoking my cigarette. I was seventeen.

One night my eye was caught by a familiar-looking word on the spine of a book. The title was *450 Years of Chicano History in Pictures*. On the cover were black-and-white photos: Padre Hidalgo exhorting Mexican peasants to revolt against the Spanish dictators; Anglo vigilantes hanging two Mexicans from a tree; a young Mexican woman with rifle and ammunition belts crisscrossing her breast; César Chávez and field workers marching for fair wages; Chicano railroad workers laying creosote ties; Chicanas laboring at machines in textile factories; Chicanas picketing and hoisting boycott signs.

From the time I was seven, teachers had been punishing

me for not knowing my lessons by making me stick my nose in a circle chalked on the blackboard. Ashamed of not understanding and fearful of asking questions, I dropped out of school in the ninth grade. At seventeen I still didn't know how to read, but those pictures confirmed my identity. I stole the book that night, stashing it for safety under the slop-sink until I got off work. Back at my boardinghouse, I showed the book to friends. All of us were amazed; this book told us we were alive. We, too, had defended ourselves with our fists against hostile Anglos, gasping for breath in fights with the policemen who outnumbered us. The book reflected back to us our struggle in a way that made us proud.

Most of my life I felt like a target in the cross hairs of a hunter's rifle. When strangers and outsiders questioned me I felt the hang-rope tighten around my neck and the trapdoor creak beneath my feet. There was nothing so humiliating as being unable to express myself, and my inarticulateness increased my sense of jeopardy, of being endangered. I felt intimidated and vulnerable, ridiculed and scorned. Behind a mask of humility, I seethed with mute rebellion.

Before I was eighteen, I was arrested on suspicion of murder after refusing to explain a deep cut on my forearm. With shocking speed I found myself handcuffed to a chain gang of inmates and bused to a holding facility to await trial. There I met men, prisoners, who read aloud to each other the works of Neruda, Paz, Sabines, Nemerov, and Hemingway. Never had I felt such freedom as in that dormitory. Listening to the words of these writers, I felt that invisible threat from without lessen—my sense of teetering on a rotting plank over swamp water where famished alligators clapped their horny snouts for my blood. While I listened to the words of the poets, the alligators slumbered powerless in their lairs. Their language was the magic that could liberate me from myself, transform me into another person, transport me to other places far away.

And when they closed the books, these Chicanos, and went into their own Chicano language, they made barrio life come alive for me in the fullness of its vitality. I began to learn my own language, the bilingual words and phrases explaining to me my place in the universe. Every day I felt like the paper boy taking delivery of the latest news of the day.

Months later I was released, as I had suspected I would be. I had been guilty of nothing but shattering the windshield of my girlfriend's car in a fit of rage.

Two years passed. I was twenty now, and behind bars again. The federal marshals had failed to provide convincing evidence to extradite me to Arizona on a drug charge, but still I was being held. They had ninety days to prove I was guilty. The only evidence against me was that my girlfriend had been at the scene of the crime with my driver's license in her purse. They had to come up with something else. But there was nothing else. Eventually they negotiated a deal with the actual drug dealer, who took the stand against me. When the judge hit me with a million-dollar bail, I emptied my pockets on his booking desk: twenty-six cents.

One night in my third month in the county jail, I was mopping the floor in front of the booking desk. Some detectives had kneed an old drunk and handcuffed him to the booking bars. His shrill screams raked my nerves like a hacksaw on bone, the desperate protest of his dignity against their inhumanity. But the detectives just laughed as he tried to rise and kicked him to his knees. When they went to the bathroom to pee and the desk attendant walked to the file cabinet to pull the arrest record, I shot my arm through the bars, grabbed one of the attendant's university textbooks, and tucked it in my overalls. It was the only way I had of protesting.

It was late when I returned to my cell. Under my blanket I switched on a pen flashlight and opened the thick book at random, scanning the pages. I could hear the jailer making his rounds on the other tiers. The jangle of his keys and the sharp click of his boot heels intensified my solitude. Slowly I enunciated the words . . . p-o-n-d, ri-pple. It scared me that I had been reduced to this to find comfort. I always had thought reading a waste of time, that nothing could be gained by it. Only by action, by moving out into the world and confronting and challenging the obstacles, could one learn anything worth knowing.

Even as I tried to convince myself that I was merely curious, I became so absorbed in how the sounds created music in me and happiness, I forgot where I was. Memories began to quiver in me, glowing with a strange but familiar intimacy in which I found refuge. For a while, a deep sadness overcame me, as if I had chanced on a long-lost friend and mourned the years of separation. But soon the heartache of having missed so much of life, that had numbed me since I was a child, gave way, as if a grave illness lifted itself from me and I was cured, innocently believing in the beauty of life again. I stumblingly repeated the author's name as I fell asleep, saying it over and over in the dark: Words–worth, Words–worth.

Before long my sister came to visit me, and I joked about taking her to a place called Kubla Khan and getting her a blind date with this *vato* named Coleridge who lived on the seacoast and was *malias* on morphine. When I asked her to make a trip into enemy territory to buy me a grammar book, she said she couldn't. Bookstores intimidated her, because she, too, could neither read nor write.

Days later, with a stub pencil I whittled sharp with my teeth, I propped a Red Chief notebook on my knees and wrote my first words. From that moment, a hunger for poetry possessed me.

Until then, I had felt as if I had been born into a raging ocean where I swam relentlessly, flailing my arms in hope of rescue, of reaching a shoreline I never sighted. Never solid ground beneath me, never a resting place. I had lived with only the desperate hope to stay afloat; that and nothing more.

But when at last I wrote my first words on the page, I felt an island rising beneath my feet like the back of a whale. As more and more words emerged, I could finally rest: I had a place to stand for the first time in my life. The island grew, with each page, into a continent inhabited by people I knew and mapped with the life I lived.

I wrote about it all—about people I had loved or hated, about the brutalities and ecstasies of my life. And, for the first time, the child in me who had witnessed and endured unspeakable terrors cried out not just in impotent despair, but with the power of language. Suddenly, through language, through writing, my grief and my joy could be shared with anyone who would listen. And I could do this all alone; I could do it anywhere. I was no longer a captive of demons eating away at me, no longer a victim of other people's mockery and loathing, that had made me clench my fist white with rage and grit my teeth to silence. Words now pleaded back with the bleak lucidity of hurt. They were wrong, those others, and now I could say it.

Through language I was free. I could respond, escape, indulge; embrace or reject earth or the cosmos. I was launched on an endless journey without boundaries or rules, in which I could salvage the floating fragments of my past, or be born anew in the spontaneous ignition of understanding some heretofore concealed aspect of myself. Each word steamed with the hot lava juices of my primordial making, and I crawled out of stanzas dripping with birth-blood, reborn and freed from the chaos of my life. The child in the dark room of my heart, that had never been able to find or reach the light switch, flicked it on now; and I found in the room a stranger, myself, who had waited so many years to speak again. My words struck in me lightning crackles of elation and thunderhead storms of grief.

When I had been in the county jail longer than anyone else, I was made a trustee. One morning, after a fist fight,

I went to the unlocked and unoccupied office used for lawyer-client meetings, to think. The bare white room with its fluorescent tube lighting seemed to expose and illuminate my dark and worthless life. And yet, for the first time, I had something to lose—my chance to read, to write; a way to live with dignity and meaning, that had opened for me when I stole that scuffed, second-hand book about the Romantic poets. In prison, the abscess had been lanced.

"I will never do any work in this prison system as long as I am not allowed to get my G.E.D." That's what I told the reclassification panel. The captain flicked off the tape recorder. He looked at me hard and said, "You'll never walk outta here alive. Oh, you'll work, put a copper penny on that, you'll work."

After that interview I was confined to deadlock maximum security in a subterranean dungeon, with ground-level chicken-wired windows painted gray. Twenty-three hours a day I was in that cell. I kept sane by borrowing books from the other cons on the tier. Then, just before Christmas, I received a letter from Harry, a charity house samaritan who doled out hot soup to the homeless in Phoenix. He had picked my name from a list of cons who had no one to write to them. I wrote back asking for a grammar book, and a week later received one of Mary Baker Eddy's treatises on salvation and redemption, with Spanish and English on opposing pages. Pacing my cell all day and most of each night, I grappled with grammar until I was able to write a long true-romance confession for a con to send to his pen pal. He paid me with a pack of smokes. Soon I had a thriving barter business, exchanging my poems and letters for novels, commissary pencils, and writing tablets.

One day I tore two flaps from the cardboard box that held all my belongings and punctured holes along the edge of each flap and along the border of a ream of state-issue paper. After I had aligned them to form a spine, I threaded the holes with a shoestring, and sketched on the cover a hummingbird fluttering above a rose. This was my first journal.

Whole afternoons I wrote, unconscious of passing time or whether it was day or night. Sunbursts exploded from the lead tip of my pencil, words that grafted me into awareness of who I was; peeled back to a burning core of bleak terror, an embryo floating in the image of water, I cracked out of the shell wide-eyed and insane. Trees grew out of the palms of my hands, the threatening otherness of life dissolved, and I became one with the air and sky, the dirt and the iron and concrete. There was no longer any distinction between the other and I. Language made bridges of fire between me and everything I saw. I entered into the blade of grass, the basketball, the con's eye and child's soul.

At night I flew. I conversed with floating heads in my cell, and visited strange houses where lonely women brewed tea and rocked in wicker rocking chairs listening to sad Joni Mitchell songs.

Before long I was frayed like a rope carrying too much weight, that suddenly snaps. I quit talking. Bars, walls, steel bunk and floor bristled with millions of poem-making sparks. My face was no longer familiar to me. The only reality was the swirling cornucopia of images in my mind, the voices in the air. Mid-air a cactus blossom would appear, a snake-flame in blinding dance around it, stunning me like a guard's fist striking my neck from behind.

The prison administrators tried several tactics to get me to work. For six months, after the next monthly prison board review, they sent cons to my cell to hassle me. When the guard would open my cell door to let one of them in, I'd leap out and fight him—and get sent to thirty-day isolation. I did a lot of isolation time. But I honed my image-making talents in that sensory-deprived solitude. Finally they moved me to death row, and after that to "nut-run," the tier that housed the mentally disturbed.

As the months passed, I became more and more sluggish. My eyelids were heavy, I could no longer write or read. I slept all the time.

One day a guard took me out to the exercise field. For the first time in years I felt grass and earth under my feet. It was spring. The sun warmed my face as I sat on the bleachers watching the cons box and run, hit the handball, lift weights. Some of them stopped to ask how I was, but I found it impossible to utter a syllable. My tongue would not move, saliva drooled from the corners of my mouth. I had been so heavily medicated I could not summon the slightest gesture. Yet inside me a small voice cried out, I am fine! I am hurt now but I will come back! I am fine!

Back in my cell, for weeks I refused to eat. Styrofoam cups of urine and hot water were hurled at me. Other things happened. There were beatings, shock therapy, intimidation.

Later, I regained some clarity of mind. But there was a place in my heart where I had died. My life had compressed itself into an unbearable dread of being. The strain had been too much. I had stepped over that line where a human being has lost more than he can bear, where the pain is too intense, and he knows he is changed forever. I was now capable of killing, coldly and without feeling. I was empty, as I have never, before or since, known emptiness. I had no connection to this life.

But then, the encroaching darkness that began to envelop me forced me to re-form and give birth to myself again in the chaos. I withdrew even deeper into the world of language, cleaving the diamonds of verbs and nouns, plunging into the brilliant light of poetry's regenerative mystery. Words gave off rings of white energy, radar signals from powers beyond me that infused me with truth. I believed what I wrote, because I wrote what was true. My words did not come from books or textual formulas, but from a deep faith in the voice of my heart.

I had been steeped in self-loathing and rejected by

everyone and everything—society, family, cons, God and demons. But now I had become as the burning ember floating in darkness that descends on a dry leaf and sets flame to forests. The word was the ember and the forest was my life.

I was born a poet one noon, gazing at weeds and creosoted grass at the base of a telephone pole outside my grilled cell window. The words I wrote then sailed me out of myself, and I was transported and metamorphosed into the images they made. From the dirty brown blades of grass came bolts of electrical light that jolted loose my old self; through the top of my head that self was released and reshaped in the clump of scrawny grass. Through language I became the grass, speaking its language and feeling its green feelings and black root sensations. Earth was my mother and I bathed in sunshine. Minuscule speckles of sunlight passed through my green skin and metabolized in my blood.

Writing bridged my divided life of prisoner and free man. I wrote of the emotional butchery of prisons, and of my acute gratitude for poetry. Where my blind doubt and spontaneous trust in life met, I discovered empathy and compassion. The power to express myself was a welcome storm rasping at tendril roots, flooding my soul's cracked dirt. Writing was water that cleansed the wound and fed the parched root of my heart.

I wrote to sublimate my rage, from a place where all hope is gone, from a madness of having been damaged too much, from a silence of killing rage. I wrote to avenge the betrayals of a lifetime, to purge the bitterness of injustice. I wrote with a deep groan of doom in my blood, bewildered and dumbstruck; from an indestructible love of life, to affirm breath and laughter and the abiding innocence of things. I wrote the way I wept, and danced, and made love.

Past Present

When I finished my last prison term twelve years ago, I never dreamed I would go back. But not long ago I found myself looking up at the famous San Quentin tower as I followed an escort guard through the main gates. I should have been overjoyed since this time I was a free man, the writer of a film which required a month of location-shooting there. But being there had a disquieting effect on me. I was confused. I knew that I would be able to leave every night after filming, but the enclosing walls, the barbed wire, and the guards in the towers shouldering their carbines made old feelings erupt in me. While my mind told me I was free, my spirit snarled as if I were a prisoner again, and I couldn't shake the feeling. Emotionally, I could not convince myself that I was not going to be subjected once more to horrible indignities, that I would not have to live through it all again. Each morning when the guards checked my shoulder bag and clanked shut the iron door behind me, the old convict in me rose up full of hatred and rage for the guards, the walls, the terrible indecency of the place. I was still the same man who had entered there freely, a man full of love for his family and his life. But another self from the past reawakened, an imprisoned self, seething with the desire for vengeance on all things not imprisoned.

As I followed the guard, passing with the crew and the actors from one compound to another, a hollow feeling of disbelief possessed me and I was struck dumb. The grounds were impeccably planted and groomed, serene as a cemetery. Streamlined circles of flowers and swatches of smooth lawn rolled to trimmed green margins of pruned shrubbery, perfectly laid out against the limestone and red brick cellblocks. But I knew that when you penetrated beyond this pretty landscaping, past the offices, also with their bouquets of flowers, past the cellblock's thick walls, there thrived America's worst nightmare. There the green, concealing surface lifted from the bubbling swamp, a monster about to rise from its dark depths. There writhed scaly demons, their claws and fangs primed for secret and unspeakable brutalities.

Even within those walls, the free man that I am eventually found himself able to forgive the sufferings of the past. But the convict in me was inflamed by everything I saw. It was all so familiar, so full of bitter memory: the milk-paned windows and linoleum tiles of the offices, the flyers thumbtacked to cork boards on the walls; the vast lower yard, and the great upper yard with its corrugated shed pocked with light-pierced, jagged bullet holes; the looming limestone cellblocks. The thought of the thousands of human beings whose souls were murdered here in the last hundred years made my blood run cold. The faintly humming body energy of six thousand imprisoned human beings bored a smoking hole in my brain. And through that hole, as if through a prison-door peephole, I saw all the free people going about their lives on the other side, while my place was again with the convicts. Anyone opening that door from the other side must die, or be taken hostage and forced to understand our hatred, made to experience the insane brutality that is the convict's daily lot, and that makes him, in turn, brutal and insane.

Since I was acting in the film, I had to dress out daily in banaroos, prison-issue blue denims. I was made up to look younger than I am, as I might have looked in 1973. After this outer transformation, I seemed more and more to become the person I had left behind twelve years ago, until finally that former self began to consume the poet and husband and father who had taken his place. I didn't know what was happening to me.

Dragged back into dangerous backwaters, I encountered my old demons. The crew seemed to sense this and gave me a wide berth. The familiar despair and rage of the prisoners was like a current sucking me down into the sadness of their wasted lives. The guards who paced the cellblocks now were no different from the guards who had leered and spit at me, beaten and insulted me. Even though I knew that now I wouldn't have to take their shit and that now I could speak up for the cons who had to hold their tongues, part of me was still caught in this time warp of displacement.

When we went to the recreational building, where I was to choose some of the convicts to act as extras, I was surprised by how young they were. I realized I was now the old man among them. In my prison days, the convicts had always seemed to be grizzled older guys, but now, for the most part, they were young kids in their twenties. After I selected the group of extras, I explained to them that the movie was about three kids from East L.A., one of whom goes to prison. As I spoke, my convict stance and manners came back to me, and the old slang rolled off my tongue as if I had never left. Memories of my own imprisonment assailed me, dissolving the barrier between us.

Although technically I was free, that first week I used my freedom in a strange way, venting hatred on anyone who looked at me, the cons included, because they, too, in the prison world, are joined in their own hierarchy of brutality.

One day a documentary crew came to where we were filming in the weight pit and asked to interview me. Prisoners of every race were present. I looked around me and was filled with contempt for every living soul there. After repeatedly refusing to speak, while microphones were shoved in my face, I suddenly decided to answer their questions.

How did I feel about returning to a prison to help film and act in this movie I had written? Was I proud and pleased? I sat on a bench-press seat curling about thirty pounds as I spoke.

I said I hated being back and that no movie could begin to show the injustices practiced here. I said that fame was nothing weighed against the suffering and brutality of prison life. I told them that these cons should tear the fucking walls down and allow no one to dehumanize them in this way. What were my feelings about being here?

I said that I hated everyone and just wanted to be left alone, and fuck them all. Just leave me alone!

I got up and walked away. There was a terrible tearing wound in my heart that I thought no one could see. But Gina, the associate producer, came up to me weeping, pleading for me to come back to myself, to be again the man she knew. She hugged me. One of the actors also approached and talked to me quietly. In spite of their attempts to comfort me, I felt helplessly encaged by powers I couldn't vanquish or control. I was ensnared in a net of memories. When the few convicts who had been hanging with me started to put some distance between us, I felt as if no one could see me or hear me. I was disoriented, as if I had smashed full force into some invisible barrier.

After a couple of days, I came out of it, dazed and bewildered, shocked and weak as if after major surgery. People I previously couldn't bring myself to speak to, I spoke with now. I felt that sense of wonder one feels after a narrow escape from death.

As I continued to live my double life, I became a keen observer of both worlds. On the streets people could cry freely, but in prison tears led to challenges and deep, embittered stares. In prison no one shakes hands, that common gesture of friendship and trust. The talk never varies from the subjects of freedom and imprisonment, the stories and the laughs are about con jobs and scams. Outside everything is always changing, there are surprises, and you talk about that. But in prison the only news is old news. It is a dead land, filled with threat, where there is no appeal from the death sentence meted out for infractions of the convict code. Imagine being hunted through the jungles of Nam day after day for twenty years, and that will tell you a little of what prison is about.

The days went by. When we finished filming, late in the evenings, I would go back to my trailer, change into my street clothes, and walk alone across the lower yard. The dead exercise pit, where many of the men spend a lot of time buffing themselves out, looked forlorn. It was very late as I crossed the lower yard to a waiting van, but the lights around the lower yard, huge, looming, twenty-eyed klieg lights, made it seem like daytime. Everything about prison life distorts reality, starting with the basic assumption that imprisonment can alter criminal behavior, when the truth is that it entrenches it more firmly. Confinement perverts and destroys every skill a man needs to live productively in society.

As I walked on, my mind full of these thoughts, buses from all over California pulled up in the eerie yellow light, disgorging new inmates who were lined up to get their prison clothes before being marched off to the cellblocks. A van was waiting to take me back to my corporate-paid condo, where there was fresh food waiting for me, where I could relax and phone my wife, turn on some soft music and write a little, read a little, in the silence; walk to the window and smell the cool night air and look across the bay to the Golden Gate Bridge and beyond to San Francisco, a city as angelic at night as any heavenly sanctum conjured up in medieval tapestries.

But all of these anticipated pleasures only intensified my anguish for those I was leaving behind, for those imprisoned who have—nothing. The cells in San Quentin's Carson block are so small that a man cannot bend or stretch without bruising himself against some obstacle. And two men share each cell. The cellblocks stink of mildew and drying feces. The noise is a dull, constant, numbing beating against the brain. Had I really inhabited such a cell for seven years? It didn't happen, it couldn't have happened. How did I survive? Who was that kid that lived through this horror? It was me. Since that time I had grown, changed; but I was still afraid to touch that reality with my mind, that unspeakable pain.

On those lonely night walks into freedom, the tremendous grief and iron rage of the convict revived in me. The empty yard, with its watchful glare, mercilessly mirrored the cold, soul-eaten barrenness of those confined within. In the world outside, convicts have mothers and wives and children, but here, in this world, they have nothing but the speed of their fists. They have only this one weapon of protest against the oppression of brain-dead keepers who represent a society whose judicial standards are so disparate for rich and poor.

When a man leaves prison, he cannot look into the mirror for fear of seeing what he has become. In the truest sense, he no longer knows himself. Treated like a child by the guards, forced to relinquish every vestige of dignity, searched at whim, cursed, beaten, stripped, deprived of all privacy, he has lived for years in fear; and this takes a terrible toll. The saddest and most unforgivable thing of all is that most first-time felons could be rehabilitated, if anyone cared or tried. But society opts for the quickest and least expensive alternative—stark confinement, with no attempt at help—that in the future will come to haunt it.

Each day that we filmed at San Quentin, where I was surrounded by men whose sensibilities were being progressively eroded by prison society, the urge grew in me to foment a revolt: tear down the walls, herd the guards into the bay, burn down everything until nothing was left but a smoldering heap of blackened bricks and molten iron. And I was filled with a yearning to escape, to go home and live the new life I had fought so hard to make. The two worlds I inhabited then were so far apart I could find no bridge between them, no balance in myself. My disorientation was radical.

My days were spent in this prison, among men who had been stripped of everything, who had no future; and of an evening I might find myself in the affluence of Mill Valley, attending a ballet with my visiting wife and two sons, my wife's cousin's daughter dancing on stage in a mist of soft lights. . . .

As the weeks passed, I realized I had gone through changes that left me incapable of recognizing my own life. What was most shocking to me was not that I had survived prison, but that the prisons still stood, that the cruelty of that life was still going on; that in San Quentin six thousand men endured it daily, and that the system was growing stronger day by day. I realized that America is two countries: a country of the poor and deprived, and a country of those who had a chance to make something of their lives. Two societies, two ways of living, going on side by side every hour of every day. And in every aspect of life, from opportunities to manners and morals, the two societies stand in absolute opposition. Most Americans remain ignorant of this, of the fact that they live in a country that holds hostage behind bars another populous country of their fellow citizens.

I do not advocate the liberation of murderers, rapists, and sociopaths. But what of the vast majority of convicts, imprisoned for petty crimes that have more to do with wrong judgment than serious criminal intent or character defect? They are not yet confirmed in criminality, but the system makes them criminals. Society must protect itself against those who are truly dangerous. But they comprise only a small proportion of our prison population.

One day, late in the afternoon after we had shot a riot scene, the cellblock was in disarray: burning mattresses, men screaming, hundreds of cons shaking the bars with such force that the whole concrete and iron cellblock groaned and creaked with their rage. The cons were not acting. The scene had triggered an outrage waiting to be expressed. Finally, all that was left were a few wisps of black smoke, the tiers dripped water, and hundreds of pounds of soaked, charred newspapers were heaped on the concrete. Clothing and bed sheets, shredded to rags, dangled from the concertina wire surrounding the catwalks.

Quiet fell, the kind of dead quiet that comes after hundreds of men have been venting their wrath for hours, cursing and flailing and threatening. The smoldering trash on the cellblock floor testified to a fury that now withdrew, expressing itself only in their eyes. One of the convicts walked over to me through the silence. He told me that another convict wanted to speak with me, and led me to a cell that was in total darkness, where he spoke my name. A voice from the top bunk replied. I heard the man jump from the bunk to the floor and come to the bars. He was a tall, young Chicano with a crew cut, whose eyes were white orbs. He lived in the absolute darkness of the blind, in this small cell no bigger than a phone booth. In a soft voice he told me he had a story to tell, and asked my advice. He wanted his story to go out into the world, in print or on film.

Never has a man evoked from me such sympathy and tenderness as this blind warrior. It was plain to me that he had suffered terribly in this man-made hell, and that, somehow, his spirit had survived. I knew that his courage and his heart were mountains compared to the sand grains of my heart and courage. From behind the bars, this tall, lean brown kid with blind eyes told me how, after the guards had fired random warning shots into a group of convicts, he found himself blinded for life. I looked at him and saw the beautiful face of a young Spanish aristocrat who might be standing on a white balcony overlooking a garden of roses and lilies at dawn. I could also see in him the warrior. How softly he spoke and how he listened, so attentive to the currents of sound.

Blind Chicano brother of mine, these words are for you, and my work must henceforth be a frail attempt to translate your heart for the world, your courage and *carnalismo*. While the world blindly grabs at and gorges on cheap titillations, you go on in your darkness, in your dark cell, year after year, groping in your imagination for illumination that will help you make sense of your life and your terrible fate. I couldn't understand you. I could only look at you humbly, young Chicano warrior. You spoke to me, spoke to me with the words and in the spirit in which I have written my poems. Looking at you, I reaffirmed my vow to never give up struggling for my people's right to live with dignity. From you I take the power to go on fighting until my last breath for our right to live in freedom, secure from the brutality in which you are imprisoned. From your blind eyes, I reimagined my vision and my quest to find words that can cut through steel. You asked me to tell your story. I promised I would.

Today, as I was writing these words, a sociologist consulting on the movie led me to a viewing screen to see the eclipse: July 11th, 1991, 11:00 A.M. I looked through the shade glass and saw the sun and moon meet. I thought of you, my blind brother, and how our eyes met, yours and mine, dark moons and white suns that touched for a moment in our own eclipse, exchanging light and lives before we parted: I to tell my people's stories as truly as I can, you to live on in your vision-illuminated darkness. And I thought how the Mayans, at the time of eclipse, would rekindle with their torches the altar flame, bringing the temples to new light; how their great cities and pyramids came out of darkness and they journeyed to the sun in their hearts, prepared to live for another age with new hope and love, forgiveness and courage. The darkness again gave way to the light, and I thought of you in your darkness, and of myself, living in what light I can make or find; and of our meeting each in our own eclipse and lighting the altar flame in each other's hearts, before passing on in our journeys to give light to our people's future.

Copies of my books that I had ordered from New York arrived in San Quentin on the last day of filming. I signed them and handed them out to the convicts who had helped us. As they accepted these books of my poems, I saw respect in their eyes. To me, I was still one of them; for them, I was someone who had made it into a free and successful life. This sojourn in prison had confused me, reawakening the old consuming dragons of hatred and fear. But I had faced them, finally, and perhaps I will be a better poet for it. Time will tell.

The next morning, I woke up early and packed my bags. Then I went back to San Quentin for the last time. The production company vans and trailers, the mountains of gear, the crew and the actors, were gone. I made my way across the sad and vacant yard to make my last farewells. This final visit was a purposeful one: I would probably never set foot in a prison again. I was struck with pity for those who had to stay, and with simple compassion, too, for myself: for the pain I had endured in this month, and for that eighteen-year-old kid I once was, who had been confined behind walls like these and had survived, but who would never entirely be free of the demons he met behind bars. This last pilgrimage was for him, who is the better part of me and the foundation for the man I am today, still working in the dark to create for my people our own unique light.

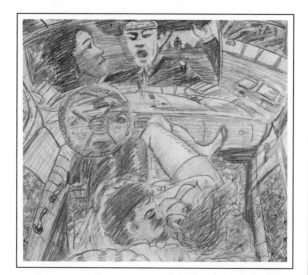

II
Working
the Dark

Working in
the Dark

As a child I watched the grownups around me plough through uncharted darkness with primordial innocence. They were wandering in a strange world that had outlawed their culture and distorted their history. They had lost control of their lives; the measuring string to make a level foundation had snapped, the surveyor's scope shattered, the center pole cracked. In the fifties, Chicanos began to search in the darkness for the light that would define their identity. I inherited that journey into darkness, the task of creating light by plunging into the darkness of the heart to retrieve our soul's name.

My people were searching for the seventh cave of Aztlán, where legend says we come from, looking for symbols to orient themselves in the world. But they found none. I remember hearing my grandmother and grandfather whispering to each other, *"No hay con que, no hay con que"*: There is not enough to go around, not enough. Many died of this anxiety. Traditional customs and values were abandoned for foreign Anglo customs. Around hearth fires Chicanos shared their sense of futility. At dances and rodeos they drank and fought, pueblo against pueblo. The great exodus into darkness had begun.

Paralysis set in, a grumbling hush of discontentment filled our house, and warnings of impending violence. English infiltrated Spanish; secrecy, mistrust and coded language marked the most casual conversations. People left rural towns for the cities, abandoning their homes to the predators who descended on farms and ranches to scavenge cheap land and the hand-hewn antiques that had furnished our homes.

I shared in my people's despair. But their suffering and the shattered hopes that stripped them bare also exposed the innermost truth of their souls. Truth was the gift bequeathed to me by my people.

I remember hearing the men in the pueblo ask each other to stand shoulder to shoulder with them against the outsiders. Looking in the faces of these men, I would see a child's face looking out from behind the mask of maturity with pleading eyes. And in my heart I, too, swore my allegiance. I was seven.

Llano men who never left the ranch were rough, unafraid of death, surviving at the edge with scarce sustenance, caressing the earth with great humility. They were men who were unable to express emotion, and their silence showed how vulnerable they were. They emanated dignity, debauched themselves in *cantinas*, crossed themselves before a church, were fearless of work, gun or fist, and they bravely faced out the inimical climates that sought to damn them to their knees. But these men refused to live on their knees, refused to extend their palms and beg for charity; instead they poached the government forest lands to feed their families.

When the men would leave the house, I could hear their souls in the wind that swept over the prairie, growling full of rancor, battling the devil out there somewhere, in the mountains or *arroyos* or plains. Shooting off their guns and swinging their axes, attacked and cursed by forces they could not touch or see, they were willing to die for a final confrontation with their inner darkness. They demanded strength from the darkness in their hearts.

For the child I was, left behind, the cold linoleum and embering ashes in the iron stove at dawn, the tang of wet spruce and coffee, spread a comforting fragrance through the house. The sharpness of dried sweat mingled with the detergent smell of freshly starched work shirts. The floors were always impeccably swept and the cupboards and counters scoured of crumbs, the few furnishings placed with utmost care. Cleanliness in the house served as bulwark against the chaos of the world outside the door. As long as images of San Martín and the bleeding Sacred Heart of Christ were nailed to the wall, the insane world could be endured. There was refuge in this order, preparedness for God's help to come.

The women in my family had a beauty like that of transparent streams. But they were powerfully sensual too, their laughter voluptuous jazz notes, and they swayed on shotgun trigger-sprung hips. Their bodies, their hair and their breasts gave off a flowery heat.

But then a darkness set in, and the center of their beauty hardened and cracked. After the day's hard labors, their fingers coiled inward like black scorpions ready to strike. They drove tractors, bucked hay, tussled with calves in the corral, whistled in horses from the field, and steered teams of mules across the sun-cracked tracts of prairie. They swigged tequila from the bottle, and when they made love, with arched pelvis and wrenching hips, they were mean enough to make a man beg for mercy.

They could lie with a smile and silence objections with a glance, but they could not defend themselves from the gnawing despair in their hearts. Darkness devoured them, and the perfume of remorse scented their skin. I watched their beauty tenderly ripen—and then harden and wither, destroyed by labor and hardship, until light could no longer pass through the jewel of their heart.

Angelic at dawn, the men and women I grew up among exploded into viciousness by nightfall. Until at last they lay together in shared exhaustion, spent and breathing hard not from fulfillment but from the weight of the yoke of captivity.

I saw the darkness wrestle my father down. Some nights he would come home crazily babbling about all the things he wanted to get for me, do for me. And then he would weep and curse that none of his dreams for me could be fulfilled. Sometimes my mother would shriek helplessly like a wild animal caught in a trap. After such times, they would be overcome by lethargy, fall silent, and stare at each other with hate.

I inherited this darkness. I am familiar with the ax and hoe, the obdurate silence of dirt that blisters my working hands. Each wound in me is a niche where icon saints champion pain, offering no way out but dreams of heaven. I caress the shovel handle as if it were a child's head whose hair I lightly tousle.

And this dark destiny formed my character. I am the man who didn't want to come home because domestic life was bad, the bill collectors waiting, the future bleak; and I drank to get the devil out of me. And when I spoke, my words left a dark mist on the air.

But darkness is that part of me from which I channel truth into my words, words like a virgin's first blood that stains the white sheets in lovemaking. It demands that I drink from life's bitterness, choking on the nauseous flavor. I hear the ancient resonance of Aztec drums in the stone-floor square, a language of the dead that cracks tombstones and flowers up out of the dirt, and I am consumed in fiery song. Words taken from the darkness are like birth-pain utterances. The sun wants a sacrifice and darkness wields a knife at my heart.

The language of barrio life is made of elemental images. Two birds clash in midair; a man snaps his fingers to a song of love won and lost; and the earth trembles, souls change in the daylight dark. This is the poetry I mine, of my people and my place.

My words like spirit-sticks tap out songs, calling upon the darkness to evoke the spirits of our Chicano ancestors— Mayan, Olmec, Aztec, Mexican—and to make of their musics one Chicano song. Their breath, blowing through the hollow flute-shoots of my bones, gives me the song of blue corn and Río Grande water and pinto beans and green chile . . . and *carnalismo*.

My disinherited people have mated spiritually with horse and mountain, earth and *llano* winds. They mated with the great mothering darkness from which all life comes, flowing back into it, returning to the beginning to find the light that can reveal what their new beginning will be.

We have not lost our darkness, as many cultures have. It is in that place we name ourselves Chicanos. And every bird, every rock, every glistening raindrop of our land calls our name back to us.

Darkness anchors its hook in my blood. The great anchor drags my life this way and that. I am gaffed by the flower, raked across the plains, turned over with last year's field stubble; and I arise in my song as new grass in the spring.

Imagine
My Life

One afternoon, editing video footage shot in the village where I spent part of my childhood, my grandmother's face appeared on the monitor, and shock waves of hurt erupted in me. Her image revived the unbearable pain of leaving her when I was a child. I always thought my childhood was savage, beautiful in parts, but mostly full of hurt. Seeing her face, ravaged leather cracked and burned by the sun, her silver, squash blossom eyes, it came back to me how much she had loved me and how warm and nurturing my childhood had been because of her love.

On the film, her mouth pursed into wrinkles as she said in Spanish, "You ran every day to the railroad, and no matter how we spanked and scolded you, you would run to play on the tracks. You spent so many afternoons there. You loved waving to the caboose engineers, and throwing rocks at the cattle cars to see if you could hit them between the slats. You had a fascination for things that went away, that traveled and came by in a whoosh and then were gone. You wanted to go with them and it was hard to bring you back, to bring you home, especially after you had seen a train. You wanted to go after those trains and I was scared when you ran alongside them. Once you threw your rosary on top of one of those flat cars and waved it good-bye. Yes, how you loved things that ran and went on and on."

I didn't remember any of that. It hurt to have forgotten

so much, and I wondered why I had imagined my life so destitute and deprived.

My grandmother had an old-world decency. She would offer food first to the guest, offer the best chair, offer whatever the guest lacked: comfort, a bed, change from her penny purse. She would share anything she had, listen in consoling silence for hours, give of herself unstintingly, and pray every night for those less fortunate than she. I would fall asleep to that mumbling drone of prayers, like a Buddhist monastery chant. They calmed me and I fell into tranquil dreams.

My grandmother's face has a powerful dignity, like that of an old female eagle on a craggy peak, whose world is eternal. Her gestures are restrained, tentative and soft, as if the world around her, the innocent earth and flowers, were a child easily bruised. Her silence is sunlight sparkling in a freshwater snowmelt stream.

The memories of her suffering, evoked by those film images, were too much for me. I stopped the monitor, pulled on my oilskin jacket and left the house. As I walked, a dark remorse brimmed in me. If I had not left our village, if I had stayed all these years with her, I could have learned from her; I could have been a better man than I am today. My life seemed to me a fool's jig of drunken jesters dancing for the deaf and blind. I fled from her face because it was too strong a telling of undeserved suffering. As I thought these things, my rage burst out in savage sounds of grief.

Those who cannot see might take my grandmother's kindness and caring for weakness. She has lived with hunger—beans, tortillas and chile her daily bread; worn frayed and faded clothes, mended a thousand times over. Yet never has she extended her hands for help, those hands always reaching to help others. For more than eighty-five years she has risen before daybreak to prepare the breakfast for her family. Her meals are offerings of the highest graces from her heart—food like spring flowers, to those who know how to savor the fragrant scents of fermenting earth and the magic of dew and sunlight. Her aged body is bent as if in perpetual homage to the earth. Those aspects of goodness that she embodies—truth, kindness, giving, and compassion—are virtues of high wisdom that the hurrying world derides.

I wish I had sat with her longer to listen to the stories of the history of our people that she carried inside her frail rib cage as a morning dove carries the song that awakens dreamers to the dawn. On rare visits after I left home, we would sit in her kitchen, happy to be together, and I would make her laugh, so hard she would cry, at my *vato loco* jokes, pulling her handkerchief from her sleeve and dabbing her wrinkled cheeks. She loved my wordplay. To her I was still the little boy who obeyed no one, who after getting spanked would rush to a grownup's knees and hug them, who needed to be loved and was afraid to love. I was still the angel who tripped over his wings and loved running more than being still and good, who loved laughter and men's conversations in bars more than prayers in church.

When I would tell her how difficult it was to pay my bills, she would smile gently and say, "Poverty in the pockets brims riches in the imagination, that's why you are a poet."

Those images of my grandmother's anguished face impacted the deepest reserves of my feelings and made me understand the misery of her life as something criminal. How distant she is from my world, how much truer and more sustained is her world in grounded work of the spirit. As I mourned the distance, it seemed as if my life, a boat halfway across the lake, was capsizing.

Yet as a child I had lived in her world and drawn from her spirit, the mirror that gave me my face. When I was near her, I too was gentle and caring, and raucous with joy as a yearling colt cavorting on canyon slab rocks, outrunning the wind. With gusto and reverence, I lapped up hot chile and bean soup, slurped the goat's milk that fed my young strength. Leaping up from the table, I would roll on the ground, intoxicated with laughter.

In those early days, I used to watch the men of our barrio build adobe and clapboard houses for neighbors, how their hands worked the earth with love, with such dignified attention to their tasks. The rigors of life were themselves occasions of praise for the sustaining life-force that allowed us to breathe and wake and work. Work became a celebration of hands, of fingers that could move and bend, grip and push. Intelligence, wood, mud, voice, eye, were all precious, all gifts, but laughter was the highest gift, and courage and endurance. When the men worked there was much laughter, but long spells of silence, too, before the talk would start up again, so quietly. They did with words what Bach could do with musical notes: they composed the most beautiful improvised poems from everyday talk. And, as I listened, the red seed of my young heart took root and blossomed under the prairie moon.

These men always followed careful pathways through their days, following ways where they would not be obstructed, avoiding foreigners who might question them or block their passage. They refused promotions that would compromise their cultural values, preferring to work with friends and earn less than to work with strangers at a higher status and wage. Work of the hands, with the earth, was to them holy work, good for the spirit, that allowed a man to feel his life lived on earth was shared with others. And there is much good to say about leaving your house at dawn, in your trusty jacket and breathing in the cold air, walking down a familiar path to meet friends who wait for you, noticing the changes in the fields around you, and feeling the rising sun on your cheeks and brow.

It was a mythic life they lived. Yet these gentle heroes were regarded as ignorant and vicious by those who did not know their hearts. Outsiders provoked them to fight to enhance their own machismo. They treated these kind men as if they were knife-carrying savages, every one, against whom you had to strike the first blow. When they came around looking for trouble, or arrogant tourists snooped around our yard, my uncles would ask them politely to leave. But then, if they still hung around, treating the place as if it was their own, my uncles would get angry. Without a word they would lift these intruders off the ground and toss them into the pickup bed, or drag them out of the yard by the collar and throw them in the dirt road.

The time came for me to leave the pueblo and go to school. There I learned hard lessons not to be found in books. The Anglo boys mocked me and hurled insults at me. I felt ashamed and lowered my head, trying to hide my face. When they beat me up they were heroes; but when I struck back, defending myself and knocking them down, I got the name of troublemaker. Their blows boosted their self-esteem, while, for a time, my defenseless silence assured my survival.

Looking at the monitor, hearing my grandmother talk and seeing her gestures, brought back to me what I had lost. Because I was too fragile and sensitive to endure the abuse, eventually I struck back. And, in so doing, I lost the inner balance of my elders, rejecting their wisdom and becoming lost to their ways.

At first I withdrew into silence, searching out others like me, brown children from rural towns whose confidence had been crushed; outsiders, unwanted, scorned, and condemned to lives of servitude. But later I rebelled, refusing to do anything I was told to do. Yet fighting was against my deepest instincts. When I raised a fist, my other hand stretched out, pleading for peace. I was caught in a conflict not of my making, that squeezed from me every drop of my childhood's sweetness.

I soon realized that, to many, I was just a *mestizo* boy destined for a life of hard work in the fields or mines, and nothing more. But that was a judgment I couldn't accept. Knowing no other way to refuse, I found myself falling into the dark worlds where the winos and ex-cons live, a gypsy child in the urban wasteland, hanging under neon lights and on hopeless street corners. I began to drink and take drugs.

I was becoming what society told me I was—prone to drugs and alcohol, unable to control my own life, needing a master to order my affairs, unworthy of opportunity and justice—a senseless beast of labor. I drugged my pain and drowned my self-hatred in drink, seeking oblivion. I had no future, no plans, no destiny, no regard for my life; I was free-falling into bottomless despair. Death seemed the only way out.

Finally, I found myself hoping for death in a fight with the police or the Anglos; or that a security guard would shoot me when I tried to rob his building. Or that one night while driving my car I'd be so high I would sail off a cliff and explode in a rage of bursting petroleum and gnarled iron, my misery ending in a smoldering, lifeless mound of pulverized bone and burning flesh at the bottom of a canyon.

Now I had become the coauthor, with society, of my own oppression. The system that wanted to destroy me had taught me self-destruction. I had become my own jailer and racist judge, my own brutal policeman. I was ruthless to myself, and murdered all my hopes and dreams. I was in hell.

They told me I was violent and I became violent, they told me I was ignorant and I feigned ignorance. It was taken for granted I would work for slave rations at the most foul and filthy jobs, and I did. It was taken for granted I could not resolve my own problems, and I relinquished control of my life to society's masters.

I was still young, a teenager, tormented because none of what I did was who I was. I was screaming for release, I was afraid. My dreams for a good life, a life I would make for myself, had been strangled at birth or were stillborn.

They sent me to prison for drug possession. And there, out of suffering, I found a reprieve from my chaos, found language, and it led me back to the teachings and conduct of my elders. I discovered a reason for living, for breathing, and I could love myself again, trust again what my heart dreamed and find the strength to pursue those dreams.

Language has the power to transform, to strip you of what is not truly yourself. In language I have burned my old selves and improvised myself into a new being. Language has fertilized the womb of my soul with embryos of new being.

When I left prison, I went to see my sister, who showed me photographs of a teenager leaning against a Studebaker, his foot on the bumper, a bottle of wine in his hand. In the background a park, mildly subdued in afternoon sunlight. It was me, my sister said, at Highland Park. I remember my amazement and pain that I had no recollection of ever being this person I was looking at.

The mistral singer I am, whose hand-clapping, heel-kicking love-dances celebrate every living moment, has always found it hard to go back home. The place of humble origins exposes the illusions of my life. My loss thunders with fountains of memories and I want to reach out to the paths, the alleys, the leaning fences, the adobe bricks, the ground and kiss them all, rub my face in the grass and inhale the sweet earth and mesquite fragrance of my innocence.

Going back, there is so much hurt to overcome.

Recently, I visited our village again. My grandmother's house there is a very lonely house, filled with spirit shadows, spiritual presences, lingering echoes of ancient drumbeats. In the yard, the golden yield of spring in all its millions of shoots are evocations of the returning dead, breaking dirt to smell and taste and bathe again in the warm sunlight.

My grandmother is hunchbacked and disfigured now with age, a bronzed anchor, her hooked fingers refusing to loosen their grip on the *llano*. Her wrinkles are encrusted watermarks on canyon walls, telling of almost a century of living. So many years after her birth, she still stands in her back doorway to welcome friends.

Pools of silence float in the rooms where her children, my uncles and aunts, once lived. People were born and grew up there and went away, leaving their spirit-prints on the air.

There is something in quiet rooms where old grandfathers and grandmothers have lived and died that vibrates with sanctity. Some of these presences do not want something to be touched or revealed. Others want something to be remembered. These spirits mourn lives filled with struggle, pain, solitude and love, mourn the moments when they felt truly one with all earth and all people. And now there is empty space, the great vertigo of nothingness, of chairs and beds, rugs and old photos, and curtains and wood and windows falling into a meaningless abyss of motionless silence.

So few things make sense to me. I have lived on the dark side of life so long, nosing my way into patches of rotting life to find my answers; the side of life where I wear my coat without sleeves, where sometimes I wake up in the morning and shave only one side of my face, where I wear a hat with a brim and no crown. I furnish my life with what I can find on the road or in trash cans—books, chairs and shoes that have known other lives, picked up by the waysides on my journey. I am fool and king, genius and imbecile, for this is what it is to be a poet. In my poems, whatever has been crippled in me, my hope and love and trust and endurance, rises again in spume of fire, unleashing bird wings and jungle howls. My poems beckon those who are dry into the rain, those without love into lovers' beds, call those who are silent to cry out and moan in revery.

Who can say why one day I take my shotgun and shoot the newspaper, bits of paper floating on the air as the little dog whines and scampers for cover? The poor telephone rings and it, too, goes up in an explosion of black plastic pieces, and I am howling and laughing. The next thing I know, I am sitting cross-legged in a tepee under a pine tree in the forest off South-14, fasting and meditating. This to me is normal.

How can I contain this violent bursting of canoes that white-water in my blood and vault into the world laden with songs and flowers? Such joy will not be confined in prisons of nine-to-five. There is too much life and too much flint in my blood, and the crazy and wild light in a boy's eyes, the innocence in a small girl's whisper, need all my life to tell and to praise.

And so my grandmother. How her image hit me with a jolt of lightning, and how her way of living, so different from mine, makes so much sense to me now, and I understand her gift to me. In her presence I can be anyone. I am a scuttling lizard scurrying from tin can to tin can, under boards, into weeds; then I jerk my praying mantis head and my right eyeball stares in one direction while my left eyeball swivels askance. My heart is a cow's tongue slowly licking a block of ice. My legs want to catch the train the way a cat catches a mouse in the cupboards. I flick on the light in the midnight of my life and cockroaches skitter everywhere on these pages, on the fingers of the reader, along the woman's dress, up the man's arm and neck and into his nose, to nest in his heart that touches the life around him with cockroach antennae, testing the floors in filthy housing projects. In the French Quarter, I am that woman at the table by a window drinking her cappuccino, her suffering concentrated in her ankles like cold iron anvils pounded with sledgehammers, her life a red-hot iron sizzling in a bucket of black water.

And on the Lower East Side, down a dingy street, in crack-dealer alleys, I howl and mutter in unknown sacred tongues. In a small mountain town in Arkansas, I am the woman screaming because her parakeet got stuck under the refrigerator and died, green shit smearing his once-sleek feathers. I am the field worker in south Texas whose showered-off dirt forms the image of Christ's face on the floor of the stall. Thousands of people arrive to pay homage to the miracle, kneeling with candles and rosaries, cripples crowding the bathroom with their crutches and braces and bottles of pills, it's a sanctuary; while the president's son in the Rose Garden snares a butterfly into his net and rips off its wings. Some day he will command great armies.

A poet in the forests of the Sangre de Cristo Mountains stares at a placid pond frozen over with crust-ice, where a bluebird flits across the steamy, cold fog simmering off the surface. And I walk out and take off my clothes and start to sing and flowers appear on the air, blue and red and green and yellow flowers, and the ice cracks and fish spin in glittering swirls and catch the flowers. And in other places millions of things are happening, equally absurd, equally heartbreaking and marvelous. How incredible our life is! How much there is that we do not understand. How honorable and full of heart has been my grandmother's life.

My grandmother does not understand what a Chicano is. She does not read newspapers, listen to radios, watch TV. Her life is lived elsewhere: thirty years meditating on the pebbles in her yard, fifty years smelling the dawn, eighty years listening to the silence at dusk, ninety years waiting for the two hummingbirds that come each spring to her unpainted picket fence—if they arrive she will live another year to await their arrival again. Forgiveness rises in her heart as she watches them whirr around the yard and hum at her screen door. She understands how they are truly flowers given wings and a beak, and how she is truly an old female turtle lumbering on wide, wrinkled footpads, raising her head with the millennial slowness of a diamond forming in the coal mines of dark years, ocean moaning in her blood vessels, returning home. While the image of a young boy chasing a train visits her, a boy as new as a just-hatched baby turtle, stumbling toward the ocean for the very first time.

A Look Back

A few years ago I went on a poetry reading tour. I was visiting two or three universities a month, sometimes as many as five or six, coast to coast. Suddenly, after living on three to five thousand dollars a year for fifteen years, I was catapulted into the comparative wealth of the national poetry forum.

Very soon I grew tired of it all. I wanted to go home and write. But at home the mailbox was stuffed with bills. Doctors and utility companies were hounding me; my two children needed clothing and school supplies. So I stayed on the treadmill, not to feed my ego but to put beans and rice and tortillas on the table. It was Alaska in winter, Mexico in summer, a dizzying ride; hopping from climate to climate, audience to audience, and for meager wages. Poets especially, and writers in general, are the most exploited artists in this country.

I arrived and departed from so many places that I would wake up in transit wondering where I was. On several occasions planes I was traveling in narrowly escaped crash-landings. Driving through impassable mountains in winter in spite of snow advisories, I saw roadbanks lined with upturned cars and jackknifed tractor trailers. Sometimes the momentum of the tour made me reckless. I kicked eighty on New York freeways, crazed from lack of sleep. I was blinded in traffic jams by the sunshine sparkling off the Pacific.

After arriving home from one reading at Yale, and saddling my horse to ride to another in the mountains of New Mexico, I thought about my destiny as a poet. At UTEP* I was accused of being a communist and narrowly escaped some murderous vigilantes. In Santa Fe, outraged by a swear word in one of the poems I read, some men in the audience started toward the stage with unmistakable intent. My friend Victor and I had to rush to our car for a quick getaway. In New York, one of the backup musicians for the reading accused me of being pornographic and refused to play, saying work like mine made a strong case for censorship.

But there were moments of rare inspiration, when poetry and audience met in transcendence, in a shared vision of love and hope.

I have no use for the pampered poets of the academy, or the darlings of fashion. Real poetry comes from and expresses the common energy of the people. Those who divorce poetry from life rob it of its redemptive power.

I have seen poetry work its magic, reducing racists and bigots to impotent rage, impelling poor women and men to weep with joy because someone has touched their hearts and expressed a little of their lives. Poetry sits in God's chair when God is absent.

So, for several years I went on reading in cathedrals and barrio community centers, in Mexican palaces and revolutionary camps in the mountains, at schools and seminaries, in hospitals to groups of dying patients and alcoholics and addicts, in prisons, on street corners. I saw what poetry could do for the human heart and soul, how it humanized and elevated earthen experience, and, if only for a moment, set the universe to rights.

And sometimes I could not contain the sorrow or joy that poetry evoked in me. I committed some despairing acts, not to fulfill the popular image of the wild-man poet, an image

---

*University of Texas at El Paso

society fosters to alleviate the guilt of dismissing poetry. I got drunk because I could not endure the madness of living in a society intent on ignoring the heart's truth. I wanted to shout at those audiences that poetry is essential to our survival, that if we lose poetry we lose what makes us human.

Poetry doesn't pay and never will pay the poet—not in hard cash. And that is as it should be. The worst thing that can happen to poets is to gain fame and financial security early in their vocation. No, the poet must pay, pay the gatekeeper dearly, with all his soul and heart, before being admitted into the Muse's presence.

Government grants and academic security are stultifying for the poet. Government should have no hand in poetry, in saying what poetry is, or validating this poet or that. The poet's work is private and lonely. He must go to the woods and fast, must edge along the precipice of society and growl at the darkness, must be fearless in facing his own demons. He must put before all else the whispering whoo-whoo of the ocean in his blood, and treat his heart like a cowrie shell, constantly listening to the sounds of his heart and the murmuring sounds of waves inside his heart that lure him to find their source in strange people, in strange places. He must challenge and confront untruth, not with muscular public outcries but through solitary discovery and humility and surrender; and by his sheer, sweating, mistake-riddled, honest search. He must approach his craft with blind faith, never knowing what to expect; abandon all control and allow the somersaulting to extremes as he walks the plank between two devouring dragons that wait at each end of the journey. Only then may he be given the verse line or flash of understanding he has searched for, that weighs no more than the sigh of a flea.

He lives for this, gives all he is for this, and it makes no sense; but he must expect no sense, and no gratitude. In making poetry you fight for your life, you fight and demand

light from Mother Earth. You plunge into the black,
thundering murk of your filth and taste all that is bitter in
yourself. You become nothing more than a shuddering
dandelion wisp in a hailstorm and you eat the thistles of your
heart, taking the knowledge of pain and transforming it into
a metaphysical black swan that floats on the page. You let
the white dove of your soul die a frozen death at your feet.
When you gouge the owl's eye out of your wisdom, groping
blindly and with aching heart through the streets of cities,
you see your life for the speck of grain it is. You let the
hummingbird take you on its course, and the river rat beneath
brown ditchwater, and the wind in rabbit holes. And you bark
and screech and laugh, a laughter filled with peace and grace
and strength, when your dreams are realized in a simple line
of verse, or the poem takes you at last to the threshold you
have sought for through twenty years of defeat and obscurity.
That is the poet's life.

Now the door has opened to your knock and you are
expected, you are not a stranger. You have come home to
a family whose lineage begins with the first human grunts
of a man and a woman feeling love, fear, hatred—and yearning
to express what they feel. Your soul merges with theirs, and
your rosy heart-wings are powdered with spring blossoms of
human sounds. Your lips and tongue are drenched in the blood
of life as a jaguar's mouth fur is matted wet after drinking
cold stream water deep in the heart of jungles.

But now let me confess. I hate poetry, I hate what it
has done to my life. It is my disease. It plagues me, whirls
me out into black zones of depression and through raging
euphorias. If I didn't have to write, I wouldn't. But for many
years poetry has been at my side, a sentry at each new road
I take in my life, and it knows me well. It is the glass through
which I see life, the respirator through which I breathe, the
counselor I take my sorrows to. It has left me sometimes

maimed and mangled, but I cannot give it up.

When I was a kid I was in love with a whore named Lolita. We lived in the same boardinghouse. Each morning I would watch her sitting on the stoop in a rough, faded skirt, her legs spread like a man, sharing Ripple or Tokay with the men who sat with her. Sitting there in the sunshine, she would paint her nails and brush out her long, thick, black hair. Her voice was cracked and deep, but to me it was like clover honey. When she drank, drops of wine would glisten on her lips and in the corners of her lips, and her tongue would dart out to catch them. Her skin had an animal fragrance. Wherever she sat was her lair, where she lived unselfconsciously, as if she were alone, a life of sparkling sadness. And yet the men came to her the way children come to an orchard of ripe apples.

I would stand across the street when she was there, doing push-ups to get her attention or leaping high to grab low-hanging branches from the elm trees. These performances always ended with my collapsing onto a nearby cinder block fence to sit and stare. Breezes tossed up the hem of her housecoat to show her calves and thighs. Sometimes the cloth that covered her breast blew aside, and for an instant I could see her breast and nipple. During those moments of forbidden revelations, the universe sounded old bells an octave deeper than any note I had known.

In the evening hours I would wait downstairs in the living room, where strange men, most of them drunk, would stumble in and ogle me, bleary-eyed. They were there to see Lolita. They mocked me when I told them she was my girlfriend. They would point at me, rocking with laughter, while I stared at them with hatred in my heart. After ten minutes in her room with one of them, Lolita would return, buttoning her blouse and jeans. Then it was the next one's turn. She would kiss his unshaven face in greeting as he passed through the milky-paned glass door, muss his oily, unkempt hair, and curl her arm around his waist as she led him to her room.

I was her dog, waiting outside the door to protect her if she needed my help, silently cursing the drunks and the suited gentlemen who came every night to visit her. I was ready to do anything she asked. As I waited, sitting in a chair on the wrong side of the door, I was assailed by tormenting images of Lolita and the man in bed: now he was suckling my woman's breast, sticking his foul tongue in her mouth, groping her ass, running his chisel-cold fingers up her legs. I could have taken a shotgun to each of them, aimed at their hearts, and pulled the trigger. Instead, later that night, I would lie in bed and masturbate to her image in my mind.

The next evening and every evening, I would faithfully return to my duty, her self-appointed guard. And Lolita would glance down at me, and the drunks once more would smirk at me as she guided their stumbling steps to her room. They would half turn and point at me and smile, shaking their heads in anticipation of private pleasure. But still to me Lolita was all the enchanting beauty that had traveled through mankind's history and been praised in song and story.

And I will tell you now that she was fat and ugly, this woman I loved so blindly, but it didn't matter. She smelled of coffee and cigarettes and vaginal juice. She ate with her fingers and bits of meat stuck to her yellow teeth; she painted herself like a circus clown and sleep crumbs stuck in the corners of her eyes. And she cursed and flipped her fingers at the men passing in the street when they mocked her. Sometimes she lifted her dress or unbuttoned her blouse for the men to see. But none of it mattered. Because, for me, she shone with a vibrant life that held me enslaved.

I would sit in the bathroom dreaming of her flesh, dream I was touching her flesh when I reached up to finger her black lace and flesh-colored panties and stockings hanging there to dry. I would close my eyes and dream we were walking with locked arms through the park. We stopped under a shade tree and I ruffled her hair. Then we were rolling together in the grass. With rugged gestures she grabbed me to her and consumed me, took me and made love to me in the sunlight, our naked bodies undulating and writhing. Then the water sprinklers showered us and we ran, naked and shimmering, chasing each other deep into the bushes, growling and biting until we wrestled each other down to make love again, in the mud and leaves and water.

I loved her in my imagination, like a man with only half a map. She was forty and I was a boy not yet into my teens. She was ugly with use, and my life was just beginning. Yet I could have died for her.

Sometimes, when I would join the group of men and women gathered on the stoop, Lolita would smile at me, take my face between her hands, and kiss my brow and cheeks. At such times her fingers felt like tongues on my skin; and as she savored my taste with her touch, she would hum with pleasure. I wanted to beg her then to make love to me, to open herself to me right there, on the hot sidewalk or the wooden porch, and love me with every bit of sharp and soft edge her love could bring.

One night a man came to visit Lolita, and when I boasted as usual that she was my girlfriend, he sensed my deeper feelings. He asked me if I had ever made love to her and I said no. He asked me if I would like to touch her. I didn't know if he was playing with me, so I looked at him and said nothing. I could feel my eyes filling with passion. *"Lo tienes, carnalito, lo tienes,"* he said: You have your wish, you have your wish. He would take her out to the backyard, he said, and lie with her there on the grass under the night sky. He told me to stay hidden in the bushes nearby, and he would signal when the time was right. I waited a little, as he asked, and then concealed myself where I could see them. He and Lolita were making out, he was kissing her. At last he motioned me to come near. He caught hold of my hand and drew it under Lolita's blouse. I felt her breast.

Lolita moaned then, and I could feel in her the female strength that wants to love and devour a man, to consume him. As my thumb and forefinger twirled softly around her nipple, feeling the dimply surface, the hot coal, she murmured something and I took fright, retreating into the bushes. A dog barked in the distance. A coyote howled on the mesa. The ghost of an old guitar player sat on the steps of the boardinghouse coaxing a mournful song from his ten-thousand-year-old guitar.

A deep sadness boiled up in me. I felt I had committed a terrible act. I had broken the love between us by crossing the boundary on the known side of which Lolita and I could still dream of each other. It was the end of a song. I had touched God's face with my hand.

I left the backyard and walked for a long while. Finally I stopped under a street lamp and opened the handkerchief I always kept with me for good luck. Knotted inside it were Lolita's nail clippings I had gathered off the stoop and hairs that had fallen from her tweezers on the bathroom sink. I shook out the handkerchief over a garden of flowers, letting all of it go. Then I sat down in the darkness, crouched under Mr. Sánchez's window, listening to the records of classical music he always played. The music told me that I would never have Lolita, never make love to her as I longed to do.

For me, Lolita filled every empty space and made things move, she gave things life by her gestures. The moon was her purple eyelid slowly concealed behind clouds and revealed as clouds passed. In my love, I was fearless. My heart opened like her lips parting to say a man's name and welcome him. I was all of those men, abased as they were; and through each of them I had held Lolita in my arms countless nights.

But one day she was gone. One of the other prostitutes

gave me a note she had written. It was drenched in perfume and carefully folded into quarters. I pressed the paper and it crackled. I smelled it and imagined I was with her wherever she was. I was dressed in a man's starched, white shirt and expensive trousers. We were walking together, her arm around my waist. She opened her umbrella in the morning sun and flocks of pigeons parted for our passage. On the lake beyond us black swans drifted. Brilliant beams of light darted off the water, and the fingers that touched Lolita's breast burned with desire as strong as a prisoner's yearning for freedom; as strong as my desire and yearning for the poem.

As I was with Lolita, so I am with poetry. I am poetry's dog. I sit in my chair while the whole world moves, and lives, and eats, and laughs, and fucks in another room. I sit apart and rage as mad-eyed strangers pass me by. Now the whole world is Lolita; and beauty is that chance breeze that lifts her dress for an instant, while I gaze upon what is forbidden to me, and desire it more than ever.

III
Portals
of Poetry

La Vida Loca*

I t's that beautiful Mexican music that understands so well a man's sadness, a man's humility, and a man's love and courage.

In prison, on torpid Saturdays, I would maybe write a letter, or call out or make hand signs to friends in the cellblock. But the pain in the soul, the twisting and slamming in my guts, like a desperate hand beating on a door; because somewhere someone is chasing the stranger and he can only find refuge behind this door, the door that never opens.

In La Pinta, in prison, you don't go anywhere. You breathe the moist rancidness of stone, of body smells, that stain prison air as nicotine stains the fingers of chain smokers, the pungency of hurt and suffering and rage. And this, Mexican music understands. I would tune my radio to a Mexican station and somehow the music drained my body of the poison fluid of grief. *Camaradas* in the cellblock would nod as I danced in my cell, writing poems in my head, bursting with images of flowery balconies and the potency of bulls in heat.

As a child, I used to go to bars with the men. There's a photograph of me in diapers, sitting on the wood floor of a *cantina* in Mexico, spinning empty miniatures of whiskey.

---

*Literally "crazy life." In this instance, it connotes the indigenous artistic sensibility as it is affected by and expresses barrio life.

And all around me old men with sweat-hardened dusty sombreros were talking and dancing. I would stare at their buckles embossed with bucking horses, bulls, or rodeo riders. They wore their jeans low, hanging from their hips, their pant cuffs crumpled on their boots; their shirts were blue or red or white, plain, simple colors. Most of them had crude, heavy rings and hefty watchbands, and crosses hung from their sun-scorched necks. Their skin was coarse from a lifetime's exposure to wind and rain, dust and heat and blowing grit.

I remember the Mexican voices that came from the jukeboxes in those places, slurred, rough, provocative voices that clawed the heart. Those passionate gasping and gripping pleas somehow exorcised my people's fears and urged them to dance and laugh and drink and seize life's pleasures, the bitter graces of their lives. And in those *cantinas* they felt a solidarity, were reassured that they had not betrayed themselves, still sustained their heart's pride.

The men and women I saw there rejected the kind of behavior that compromises dignity and bends to flattery. There was something in the way they spoke, with biblical solemnity and passionate romance, full of meaning in its simplicity, that held me.

And I fell in love with the woman in the dark corner booth, holding up her mirror to darken her luscious lips. The flashing neon sign outside the bar window would illuminate an unshaven face in another corner, and it seemed to me so handsome and exotic, this exquisitely hardened face, like a rose stiff with youth and firm with health, grown out of spring into the full height of its beauty on this one night. Tough *chucos* wearing shades, their collars turned up under snappy fedoras with dark bands and small feathers or gold pins, leaned in towards their listeners as if to conceal what they were saying. And near the bar were men and women in cowboy duds, robustly open, standing erect and tall. On the walls all around, pictures of Mexican rebels wielding pistols and embracing beautiful dark-haired women set the scene.

But of the men and women in those bars, as a child or later, I never saw their whole story, their whole life. Although I think they knew I was a friend, they peered at me as if from jungle leaves, with jaguar eyes, covert and watchful. In their faces you saw the golden-gray glossiness of eagle feathers and their sharp black shoes were eagle talons or jaguar claws that pointed when they walked, always toward Aztlán.

Late at night the gamblers would come in, impeccable in tailored suits, smelling of expensive cologne, and with dazzling women on their arms. They got up poker games, or conned the racing forms, their jeweled hands flashing money.

There were never bright lights in the life of my youth. My life was played out in the subdued lighting of small lamps and light bulbs, dim parking lights, flashlights, cigarette-lighter flames. In parking lots and on roadsides, in fields, outside darkened houses and shadowy bars, I too lived my life like a jaguar ambushed behind the dark filters of leaves. When I came to manhood, I held my woman's hand in alleys, in shadowy rooms musty with earth smells. There the couches were covered with crocheted cloths and religious pictures hung on all the walls. On little tables, good luck candles flickered before figures of Christ and the saints and bowls of hard candies. Through the always open windows, from behind blowing curtains, I would watch the sky redden and darken, studying the stars for answers to my heart's questions. Always there was that sense of being a part of everything in the universe, and always the sense that I could not find my rightful place there; that I was a coward and lost, because I was unable to tell the world who I was.

I had a car for cruising, a woman near me for loving, and Mexican music on the radio—that was my life. And all around me was this strange labyrinth called a city, not built for me. So I burned the map made for others, crumpled it and burned it in the fire, rolled my tortillas and fried me some green chile for comfort, in my room. But in the streets I was an exile looking in past doors left ajar, just a stranger passing through.

Even now, in some ways it's still the same. And puffing on my cigarette, my hands deep in my pockets, my collar up around my neck, my hat atilt—I laugh. Sometimes I warm myself at old photographs of prison friends, or photographs of my mother and father. Or, maybe, I trim my mustache and comb it out in its full scrub-brush glory. And when I walk city streets in the night, the reflection I see in the shop windows may not be me but some Pancho Villa laughing at me as he puffs on his cigar. Maybe El Francisco is with me, in the little fedora hat he always wears and his starched pink shirt, and we loiter on street corners shooting the breeze and waving at friends passing by. And maybe some woman he knows pulls over in her convertible and we have a few laughs together. And maybe we decide to pick up Eppy and Efrin and Gilbert and throw a cruise down *las calles* of our universe, and stop around midnight at Conchas for a little *menudo* or *caldo*. And while we eat we listen to Mexican music on the jukebox. Then I leave them and walk home alone, looking up at the stars from street corner pyramids, like some Mayan charting the future by the stars.

I learned my life in the kiss, in the passionate embrace, in a friend's trust, from the earth. I learned it from those people who took care of me, for a night, or a week, or a year—who taught me love. I took a little bit of each of you, *camaradas,* from your souls at their most blissful and vulnerable: from that deep and secret core that only Mexican music knows.

Groundings

After returning to Los Angeles from Kansas recently, I drove out to the beach and sat on the sand looking out at the ocean, the most powerful metaphor for our misery and our ecstasy. My visits to the ocean are curative pilgrimages. Los Angeles wears me down with all its clamor and chest-beating traffic snarls; and my film work there is stressful, the pace I keep intense. But after a little while of walking the beach, and hearing the roar-whisper of waves in my blood, I am fine, ready to plunge back into the melee of moviemaking and deals and phone calls from New York and Santa Fe.

There is something very cruel about the ocean. It strips our weaknesses bare. It is as if it knows our frivolous fancies for good foods and wines, money and power, and it sighs, knowing those things will all pass, and we, too, and our light whims will pass, even our appetite for flesh and beauty and companionship. It is sad that we who are so fleeting and mortal waste our short lives on passing things, in secret resignation to our failures and limitations, when what we remember when our lives are nearly over are those bursting moments of light when someone truly loved us the way we wanted to be loved and the way our souls are made. The only thing that lasts is the experience of such love, that perfectly filled our wants and desires, as if our souls were old grooved landscapes that a certain love came to settle in as naturally as water pools settle into pockets of rock after a rain. The voice of the ocean, too, fills a very old and deep place in me, a place like a battleground where now there is peace, but that remembers past tragedy and intolerable hurt. It loves the black, burnt craters of old wounds encrusted with rocky scabs in which golden moments of my life are embedded.

Whenever the tide rushes in, it speaks a hundred versions of my life, as old sailors freshly arrived from mysterious voyages recount to their cronies in waterfront bars tales full of dreams and horrors. And they listen, scratching their salty beards with iron-hard fingers burned blue on rope-tugging sails, sails that caught the winds that carried them forth into adventures full of fear and howling darkness.

I have looked for God everywhere in my life, and found in the melancholy man-tongue of night waves Tlaloc's moody mumbling. When I die, go tell Tlaloc how I loved him, though this desert boy from New Mexico did not know him well. Tell him my passion for his waves and the sound of waves at night; and plead with him to be my friend in the next life and grant me a destiny working my nets from a small boat and a hut within a stone's throw of the harbor. There may I wake to the cries of gulls and the voices of fishermen and sailors, to the sounds of boats coming in, going out. . . .

Like a man tossing on his bed with a fatal fever, whose mate takes a cooling cloth to his brow as he wrestles with his demons and cries out in fevered sleep, so Tlaloc gentles and cools the poet's brow of me and relieves me of some of the sickness of living in a world gorged to madness on materialism, that rejects the life of the soul.

Of those who have asked me about my life, some have prized my suffering, and others my arrogance; some my quiet meditative obsessions, and others my childish innocence. But I myself have never seen the poet in me, I have never seen clearly the face of this man who has devoted himself to poetry, enchained to its practice, who demands that writing be my life, who turned up the fortune-teller's cards commanding me to write.

When I write, creating souls in my poems, I seem to see them rise as from a burning stick, some torch in the universe; and when a given length of hairy cosmos has burned away, the ashes that fall are sucked into the loins of a man, and invisibly pass into a woman's deepest core, and there take seed. So the dreamers of the world let the burning ashes fall from their cigarettes, and so are we all, all of us, burned holes where the dust of our actions collects over a lifetime.

When people ask me, "Where does your poetry come from?," I want to answer, "Where do babies come from? What is the ignition spark that startles breath into flesh and triggers the brain's first impulse?" What is that spark, where does it come from? Who knows? Only let us celebrate that creation, for this is a mystery we will never understand. The passion to analyze is just a futile braying of our mulish egos in a stubborn belief that we can know it all. So, let us leave these unanswerable questions and celebrate the mystery.

Where does my poetry come from? I answer that I come from my poetry, I draw myself from poetry, I create myself from language, I sustain myself on poetry, I bear myself on poetry, I walk upright on two feet because of poetry. And you, reader, you take poetry from me, this cannibal who feasts on your eyes and hands and tripes, slavering over your barbaric body that, without poetry, would lack all reverence and godliness. Without poetry, you are no more than fodder, the fly-and-worm-speckled shit that starving pack dogs lick and then spew out again.

Poetry guides me to music wherein I surrender, the notes flailing and pounding and kneading me into a being of soul. Poetry breaks the silence in the just-born infant slipped from his mother's loins all bloody and slime-swamped, it is poetry's cry that screams from his lips affirming that human life will go on.

I draw my poetry from the night, from the culture of night, where our daily selves are transformed. There order becomes impulse, the public face falls away, and the face of desire smiles into mirroring glances. There silence breaks into curses and mere politeness dies; the old attic trunk is thrown open wherein we find our rage and lust, and the spoils of our secret life. In the night, all that in the life of day we would hide and deny, we don like kings assuming our rightful robes. And we reek, with pig's blood on our tongue, we wallow in the pleasant mud of our filth and decay, grunting our own abhorrent beauty. Where our civilized masks crack and we push at the borders of our primordial soul, there is the poetry I seek. The black wolf that tracks across our snowy public lives is the prey I hunt.

I rake poetry in from the ash piles, combing for the teeth and bone shards of those who died anonymous deaths on the margins of society: those who struggled for a lifetime for a loaf of bread, who lived simply and were consumed by the shame of worldly failure. And I anatomize those who hear God in them and still sin, and the rich man who buys the works of artists and never understands. I reach my bladed hands into the haunted heart of the woman made lonely by her beauty, because she is too beautiful for men to love her soul. And I search the harrowed heart of the ugly woman who kneels and weeps before her bedroom altar, because the man she loves looks at her with scorn. My poetry scrapes its claws at the bottoms of poisoned wells on whose night surface the moon glows like an empty eye socket filled with gold.

I find poetry in the man dying of cancer who still puffs his cigar and walks in the communal courtyard because he loves to be among pigeons. There is poetry when Keith Jarrett plays his music, crying out when a certain note is achieved, in vocal orgasm creaming all over the beauty of those piano sounds. There is poetry in Blind Lemon Jefferson's steel-string guitar blues, that particular tinny twang that calls up an old blackened frying pan sizzling with catfish marinated in gut-killing moonshine.

And there is poetry in old men and women in New Mexico stopping work at noon for a simple meal of chile, potatoes, and tortillas, in the sheen of sweat on their brown faces when they have eaten. Their language is like clods of earth turned by a tractor to nurture another season of crops—good dirt, brown, silent dirt, dirt that smells of the green semen of plants. Their old hearts are wicker-bone works, made of bird-wing bones; and inside those hearts are small tigers imprisoned on islands, tigers that weep and lick their wounds, and sniff the air and growl.

The kind of poetry that assaults me is tender and vulnerable as the skin beneath a turtle's shell, that fine green webbing of skin never exposed to sun or wind. Come close and breathe in its watery aroma. And now the ocean gives me these words, and the poems I make are homages I offer back to the ocean; because the ocean gave me my language, I must give it back my song. I want to make poetry carved with great patience, that resonates with many journeys, with glass staircases that shatter, burying the poet in a glimmering mountain of blood-dripping fragments sparkling with light: poetry that is both painful and ecstatic to hear and to write. My poems hold one hand in the fire, and with the other they caress a woman's sex: one hand is burned to a blackened stub, while the other keeps building pleasure. Even as you suffer to the limits of pain, you cannot stop loving the woman, the pleasure is too great, the obsession too intense, you must keep on, you too must come, consummating the ritual of love: that is my poem.

There is such faith in poets, most poems are born of sheer faith from black nothingness, an insatiable, blazing hunger for encountering what is beyond the reach of our eyes and ears, a profound appetite for death and resurrection; a rage to destroy and create anew in your own image, to partake of the mystery of your own dying and living.

And for that terrain there are no maps. For me, there were no schools, no writing workshops. But there were the voices of Neruda and Lorca, Sabines and Paz, of those men and women who cried out for the light, who in solitude begged on their knees all their lives for one word, one image, to redeem their misery and celebrate their joy, to reflect their unremitting reverence for life. Those were the voices that came to me when I was dying, whispering to me through their verse: "Do not die Santiago, you must live; even in the bleakest moments, the most severe tribulations, come clap your hands and sing, sing with us, you young poet of so little faith."

While I was in prison there were contracts out to kill me because I stood up for what I believed, protesting the abuse of my Chicano brothers. I knew without a doubt that I would die young, and no one would know that I had lived; that I would die without having uttered one word to tell the world that I had been, that I had tried my best to love and to live. But poetry lifted me to my feet and filled my heart with joy, and it was through the power of poetry that I was able to prepare myself to die, but die fighting, with courage and innocence, in defense of life.

I survived. And one day the prison gates opened and I was free. Years later, I married and my children were born. I had been a warrior for so long, but now it was time for the warrior to rest, to go to sleep forever, because my children showed me that they needed another kind of man, one who could weep and embrace and freely love. But I could not. And I had to learn again what it takes to be a poet. My children and my dreams: these were, and are, my teachers.

Many times I failed. I fled from fatherhood and fell back into old addictions, drinking and drugs. All my old self-loathing welled up in torrential bitterness and I began to court death again in my despair. I felt maimed, unable to weep or feel, hating life, hating people. Yet deep inside me the child was still alive, screaming with pain, screaming to escape from my hell, to get free, to live joyously, to love.

Isn't poetry about transformation? Isn't it about interior landscapes colliding and realigning our vision of life, readjusting our inner borders so that the very idea of borders vanishes and we are confronted with the open space of limitless possibilities?

Poetry is the journey within, a poaching into the interior territories of life and death, that changes us in proportion to the courage of our forays there. That journey begins in the landscape we were given; the place where we were born is our point of departure. New Mexico's mountains, deserts, plains and barrios, rivers and ditches, fields and yards, initiated me in my craft. When I read my poetry aloud, I draw on the familiar vigor of roosters crowing at the rising sun, or bulls mounting a cow in a spasm of bulging muscles. That's how I read my poetry in performance, because I found the craft of the poem, the dimensions of the poem, in the fields, the voice of my poetry embodied in the black stallion bucking and rearing. I see the poem's shimmer in the gloss of wheat-gold on the air and my task is to achieve that ripeness in the pages I write. I labor until words wet with saliva issue from the moist lips of darkness, drip from the tongue like ocher sap from a *piñon* branch. The mountains of New Mexico give me my craggy tones, that ache as my legs ache when I climb, and hurting words that pull against each other like the muscles of a climber in his ascent. Observing the way old backyards come to be over time, the fences put down with seeming haphazardness, but accommodated to the comforts of human use—next to this cottonwood, circling that mesquite—I try to capture this apparently random design in my poems. Instead of cleaving to strict feet and meter, I study the goat's bell and the lamb's baaing to learn the intervals between my words from their intervals between silence and sound. In the barrio, too, are rhythms and gestures of ritual gatherings I am driven to capture on the page.

At public readings, I call on my body to help express the feeling of the poem, moving my hands, letting my voice fall an octave and then rise to a higher pitch, and my face reflects the poem's grief or insanity. When I read, totally absorbed by the poem, I am not conscious of this. But other poets often have urged me not to read in this way, suggesting that it interferes with the poem's power to elucidate itself, to surge forth into its own culmination. That may be so, but I must follow what the poem is doing at that moment in my blood. For me the poem lives not only on the page, for when I read aloud I relive the poem, become the poem, as it takes and remakes my body as well as my soul.

So, when the poem is angry, I too become angry as I read, and as the poem weeps, so do I. I am no polite singer, like so many poets of the European tradition. I am myself, Chicano, and I follow the wind-swept trail of my people, and how they convey emotion and song in their rituals. I turn to my landscape of New Mexico, listen to how the wind moans, look to how the mountain carves its space in the sky. I hear that silence of terrible resonance that buzzes in the prairie, a silence filled with spirits and the passion of growing things singing their seasonal fruition. From the cries of the barrio and the silence of the prairie come my Chicano blues, an earth-shaking, heart-moaning song.

And my children resurrect the child in me, the poem sees through a child's eyes that still know that life is a mythic journey, a tale of great trials. The honesty of a child, his unwillingness to compromise, and his conviction against all odds that life can be good, can be as we wish it—that faith is what they give me, and the freshness of their emotions in seeing and imagining the world as a place of magic and awe.

I could not have written the poetry I have written if my children were not near me, for me to hear their whimpers and cries of delight mixing with the songs of birds and dogs' barkings; and I worry as I listen, about how to pay the rent, how to keep them clothed, and about their education. The substance of their lives has cut a wide swathe through my poetry, their little bodies and their ways and their humanity have fertilized my poetry and made it far more true than it would have been without them. I write with my ear pressed close to their ribs, listening to their small hearts pound, and when I finish a poem I measure its authenticity against their hearts' reality and their imagination. The voice of poetry runs steadily and faithfully in the veins of all children.

In the sea's strangeness and the familiar land, the day's brilliance and the murk of night, in the wisdom and innocence of a child's love of life, I find the poem's groundings.

Creativity

When I write, I bid farewell to myself. I leave most of what I know behind and wander through the landscape of language. I dive down like a dolphin, breaking the surface briefly to check the shoreline and submerging myself once more into the strange blue underworld of the image and of memory, my writing hand cleaving its way as naturally as the dolphin's tail-fin.

I am dead before I write, and becoming part of the poem, traveling through it, is an experience as powerful as that of the embryo coming from beyond his mother's womb, from a darkness beyond through an unbearable loneliness, to ignite his being into life. I am born through the coupling of words and my birth-cry is the poem. Words are my birth-slag. In writing I lose all sense of where I come from and who I am, and I wander, driven by the instinct of the moment, awestruck in the storm of dissolution and becoming. I am a bird fluttering in a courtyard bath; the rising sun against my face, I am the stained-glass cathedral window of La Virgen de Guadalupe. I am evening light that purples and blues the dry leaves drenched in moonlit rain, the sparkling debris swirling in matter, forming the world.

I remember how eagerly I waited each day in prison for the guard to bring the mail. Opening a letter was a feminine act, the unfolding of a blossom in spring; and sitting on my bunk to write a reply was a feminine process too, a period of gestation for the letter to come to birth, screaming and pleading for nourishment. Writing in prison is a prayer, a ritual, a sacramental act.

In prison I was lean, I was fast, and I carried myself like a knife blade. The energy inside me was feminine, raw silver swirling in the molten bowels of earth. I surveyed my life, appealing to the wounded part of me, the intimate earth part, and the gestures and words I found there nurtured the man who was tough and ready to fight. I sought that other part of myself, the receptive part, the part needing friendship and understanding. My feminine side gave power to my male side, gave me insight and courage, and a fierce nakedness of enduring humility.

One evening at dusk, as I walked the compound, the cons were lined up outside the property room, blankets rolled around their bodies to keep off the cold. To the west, a massive wall of rumbling clouds threatened rain. The biting chill pierced our denims and prison-issue brogans and we danced on the balls of our feet to get warm. Great white sails of steam billowed from the boiler room and the cauldrons groaned boiling water. Suddenly a violent knocking shook them and they wheezed and whistled out steam, clouds of steaming condensation showering everything around. The dark sky, the steam, the convicts huddled in their blue jumpsuits and blankets, the dead yard, the dull bulk of the cellblocks in the gray pallor of evening struck in me the deepest melancholy. There was never a sadder evening. Such evenings provoked in me feminine feelings of longing for a home, for a family and domesticity, for children to rear, and to teach, and to love. It was on such evenings that I was moved to forgive the world and ask the world's forgiveness.

Prison is its own city, a world built by men for men, run by men's rules and maintained by men's anger and brutish will to survive. But beneath that city is another, buried and from another age, that of the heart, man's child heart, brim with all a child's love and hate. And in this other city the rituals of survival are performed in watchful silence. The city of the prisoner's heart is feminine, while the body that carries it is that of the male warrior ready for war, primed to defend his pride at the cost of death, with staring hatred for all that breathes. Entering those gates that's what one feels: fear of never leaving alive and a chilling rage against those who have imposed this punishment.

In creativity the dualities of life collide. I become woman in my heart when I write. I dream of softness and whispered words and my thoughts become wombs; resinous, rippled tremblings undulate from my mouth and hands, my ears and palms become the pollen sacks where butterflies and bees pollinate in language. I am half man and half woman, howling and screeching my words as I write, coming with semen-slick thighs, wrestling and licking and mud-rutting the images in moon-madness, my lust on the page more vivid than any physical love. Every poem is an infant labored into birth and I am drenched with sweating effort. Tired from the pain and hurt of being a man, in the poem I transform myself into woman.

How my soul surges and swells with honey dew that I lick and lavish with my tongue and fingers, smearing the sweat of my breasts on the poem-body shimmering on the page, moving as lovers thrust and uncoil and wrap closer. All the rich, dark soil of fields erupts in my bowels of a bedding-down man giving birth to his own woman-self, to my own vaginal wrath and trembling sensitivity. My heart turns its lunar side to life, silencing the man in me; and I rub the earth against me until the orgasm shivers in feminine fulfillment. I see the child inside me and lift him up and kiss him and give him love, and let him feed off my tit and suckle the warm, red milk-blood of my veins.

Creativity makes vaginas of the poet's hands and mouth and sensitive penises of his limbs. The pulse of the poet entangles in green verse, in body sounds that spring from deep in the gut, and his pulse roars like semen throbbing for release. Colliding words rut together and the verse line flowers through his pores. His heart fills with honey from the image cradled in his ribs, and he nurses it on the black moon of ancient womanhood in his blood, recycling the old blood of manhood.

When I write, woman and man in that act, my dove self is eaten and my wolf self growls. In the poem I plant my seed and lick the birth-film from each vowel. I dance on the poem, offering up the currency of my dreams in the ethereal smoke of language, and emerge two-sexed and new. The impact of opposites shatters my borders.

Poetry's feminine power drips salt into your most secret wound. Truth assaults you, light emanates from each word; and your hard-edged male consciousness dissolves in surrender. When I awake in the poem's emptying center, a center where all things in the universe touch, I leap out of myself with a dual-sexed cry of freedom.

My soul is riddled with scars and wounds from the births of poems. Here was born the poem of the self-hating, drunken adolescent with a gun in his belt. And there the poem of the wrinkled-skinned wise man chanting prayers of love and innocence before his bedroom altar. Sometimes the travail of making poems leaves me pleading for sanity, for a simpler life, for a release from my visions. But this is not what I truly want, and I always come back to poetry. I go on dividing myself into words, arranging them to find new realities, to see beyond myself, leaning over the edge, risking and learning, never knowing the poem's outcome until I reach it. My fear is welcomed, my panic embraced, my terror is lived through, until the cosmic axle on which the soul spins tilts just so and the heart finds its true alignment. The journey into the poem makes of the poet a burning sun that gives birth to a million shadows.

There is a terrible silence in words that demands that I cross their devastating terrain, knowing I will never find what I need except by that grace that springs from the journey into chaos. In the perilous journey into the poem, language sustains the poet as breath sustains life. The privilege of poets is that they can become all things in the act of creation, everything—and nothing.

Creativity is a reconciliation that breaks the borders of gender. It reunites the masculine and feminine, which have been set against each other in false enmity.

"*Compórtate como un hombre,* Santiago." Many times growing up I heard that advice: Conduct yourself like a man. It was not an exhortation to violence, nor did it counsel stoic acceptance of indignities. What was meant, rather, was: don't betray those who love you; don't forget your family and your community; don't hurt others, cheat or lie; be decent and honorable: be a man. To be a man is to be loving, to know that your compassion is your strength.

The first time I felt myself breaking through to manhood was in prison, writing letters to a woman. The miles between us, and the fact that she was a poet, gave me the freedom to explore my relationship with women. In my letters I wrote down all my unbridled sexual fantasies. I became master and slave, animal and saint; and she replied in kind. I made love to her a thousand times through language, sometimes feeling her skin close to mine, the palpable heat coming off her words. I heard her groans and pleas, I touched her sweating thighs, and gently bit her lips.

This experience released all my feelings about sex. Once past adolescence, the sense that lovemaking is an incomparably sweet and succulent joy to offer another person was always highly tuned in me. But I almost never made advances to a woman. My culture was full of prohibitions of sexuality, and low self-esteem compounded the problem for me. I was a lonely teenager, too shy to participate in the rituals of dating, or even to have female friends. My limited experience had taught me that women were the shot-callers, the disciplinarians. Among my male friends, sex was treated as a joke, something foul and utilitarian, anything but romantic. All that mattered was the release of 'coming,' with or without a woman. Imagination would take the edge off of your horniness and then you could get on with other business. To the immature boy I was then, sex was a bleak and necessary pleasure.

I had to overcome the shame of not knowing how to talk with women, the guilt of thinking of them, when in their presence, as merely sexual creatures. When I had relations with a woman, once my mechanical lovemaking was done, I felt almost a revulsion. I only wanted to get away.

I inherited these attitudes, in large part, from my culture, which regarded everything to do with sex as bestial and degrading, even evil. According to the adults I knew growing up, those who enjoyed sex would reap the torments of everlasting hell. Believing this was a torment I endured for many years. Every sexual act drove the stake of despair deeper into my heart.

And yet, in the air I could smell the promise of oncoming rain from a land somewhere beyond, as the fragrance of sage comes to you in the desert before you see it, or the tang of the ocean from beyond the next hill. Somehow I intuited a different reality: that the long, delicious hours in bed with a woman, making love, sharing our secret thoughts, weeping together for our unfulfilled lives and broken dreams, was a sacred experience. I began to understand that making love is like making art. When you write, you transcend the limitations of your senses. Using them to the fullest, you go beyond them, tapping into pure and prehistoric powers. The words you find then are made of earth and flowers and fire, stone and gems, and they lead you into the heart's deepest realms.

When I started to write, all of the poisons of my misconceptions about sex, about women, and about my role as a man came to the surface. I had been taught that women were there merely to be possessed; that a man must not express any weakness, never admit to pain or hurt. These bitter untruths planted in my childish mind were the dragons that consumed my innocence. As I began to write, those early psychic wounds were cauterized. I began to discover my femininity through language. I discovered that I carried a child in me, the gestating poem. And new green shoots of my full inseminating maleness broke through to the light.

Our sensual energy emanates the glowing luster of living organisms. Something powerful resides in our lips and fingers, our loins and breasts, that breathes moonlight in men and sunlight in women. The union with a woman helps us, as men, to see into the dark realm of our powers. Our cries then are waterfalls, pure, brilliant, rushing waters, releasing a creativity that renews and revives us with new ways of seeing.

I must tell you that I have betrayed the trust of friends. I have neglected a sweet love. I have failed many times to water the tree that grows in the heart. But each night I dream my way back to sanity, and I awake each dawn to practice the dream, the reunion in the soul of male and female that gives us our full humanity.

Pushing Through

I was never much for taking advice, although I think that in a great many instances it would have helped. I wanted to experience everything, even at the risk of making big mistakes. I wanted to explore the interior of people's minds, to understand why they did what they did, and I wanted to find this out for myself. When anyone tried to give me advice, their words coming towards me melted away like snowflakes touching fire. My character was formed through adversity and tender hope, like initials scratched into prison walls.

Young poet, you who may read these lines, let me tell you honestly how it was with me in my youth, in the hope that it may help in your own struggle. I wanted to embrace all of life, the beautiful and the ugly, to sit with cowards and warriors and listen to them all. I never aspired to be right, or govern my life by theory, imperiously pointing at others the finger of righteousness.

I love struggle, and my wounds are the proud insignia from encounters into which I have flung myself fully, with no holding back. And this life, lived in the moment without reservation, has been packed with glittering success and bleak misfortune. I've played both, shaved the thickness from both, as a blues pianist wears down the black and white keys, as a hobo wears down the soles of his shoes with the miles.

I've looked for a place in America where I could say,

"Ah, this is it, yes, I'll settle here. I'll stay." I never came to that place, but along the way I have met with remarkable people who nourished my poems. When I am an old man looking back on my life, there'll be no regrets for roads not taken.

Don't depend on America to tell you who you are. Don't let yourself be tempted to become a mere linguist who dabbles in poetry for thrills or academic distinction. Reject the killing safety of literary workshops, of universities. Don't fear the jagged emotion, but tongue the sweet sap of your terror and joy; follow the tap-root that drives deep into your soul and touches the primal core of molten light that feeds all life in the universe.

Write to the maddened drum of your own passions, and don't let your imagination be tamed by the sterile pronouncements of critics. Let the hours cocoon in your heart and grow wings to fly across the continents of your imagination till they die at your feet.

Each true poem is a pearl-handled pistol you point at your heart. You twirl the cylinder of language and squeeze the trigger. The poem may reveal your weaknesses, but it will tell you how to live. It will bring you face to face with the truth. Real poems disarm us and lift us out of ourselves. They shoot sparks as from fire-blackened logs, and for an instant we leave the darkness and become scintillant beings.

There is a boulder suspended in the middle of me. The crude substance of which we are made, what is given to us genetically, is like a dense boulder. The exercise of creativity wears the stone down to a pebble, to dust and steam and air, volcano-breath.

A true poem is starlight that has reached earth.

I had a dream in a time when I was trying to kick the lingering effects of drug abuse. I would do okay for a month or so, but then I would start to use again. It was hard to deal the last blow to my habit.

In this dream there appeared a beautiful horse at my half-opened back door. I knew I had to go out and ride the horse, to mount it and ride it down, but it was wild. Probably I would get thrown and kicked and break a bone or two, but I had to risk it, it was my task to tame that horse by my own sheer power. But I was afraid.

As I was staring at the horse, it reared and stamped, challenging me. Then my wife appeared behind me and her eyes told me that there was another way. Stepping past me, she held the door open and lifted and extended her hand. She walked toward the horse slowly, until she had covered half the distance to where he stood. And the horse then went to meet her, uncertainly, hesitantly, until the two were face to face. My wife reached out and caressed his nose and went to his side and brushed his mane with her fingertips. He had become tame and trusting.

I knew that the dream was telling me that all my life I had taken on my problems by force, trying to change my life with force and through confrontation. But now it was time to try a different way, a deeper and more peaceful way, of love, and trust, and surrender.

As I walked out toward him, the horse lifted his head suddenly and his eyes were full of mistrustful fury. But when I reached out my hand he allowed me slowly to touch his head.

I was changed by that dream. Young poet, listen to your dreams.

In the orphanage one bright Sunday morning, the sun shone through all the dining hall windows. That extraordinary light made life seem a fairy tale for a small boy of six. Sundays were visiting days and hard for me, because I had no one to visit me. We had just come from Mass and I sat down at a table with five other boys. We fought over the bread on the platter in the middle of the table and we poured out fresh milk from a silver pitcher.

I looked out the window and saw a group of women in pretty dresses who had just arrived to visit. The thought came to me that one of them was my mother. I left the room to get a closer look, walking down the long corridors to where the guests would enter. Halfway down the hall, Sister Anna Louise stopped me and ordered me back to the dining hall. I started to obey, but as soon as I reached the loud dining hall I turned away to run back down the corridor. I was compelled to see the face of that woman, to be near her, to sniff her perfume and let my eyes devour her.

But Sister Anna Louise caught me again and, grasping my shirt to hold me still, began to beat me, flailing at my body and slapping my face until it went numb. I looked at her, and I knew she was out of control. Her face was contorted, swollen and crimson, and her eyes were blue beads of ice lit with small points of flame. She was unleashing upon me the fury of all that was unfulfilled in her. At last I went limp; and a part of myself fled to hide where no one could touch it.

I couldn't return to the dining hall. I lay crumpled on the hall tiles, dizzy and hot and bruised from the beating. But my one burning thought was that now I would not get to see the woman I hoped was my mother. That was the horrible, unacceptable reality. My whole universe fell in upon itself, black and toxic. Now I would not see, maybe never see, that woman who meant all life and all love to me.

Finding no outlet for my rage, I spent years in a drug-haze, endless lost days of drug-taking, crazy partying. In our drug-blitzes, all things straight and good were branded by my friends and me as hypocrisy, to us the worst of sins. We created our own distorted code that reversed the order of the universe. We believed that our suffering gave us that license.

In the drug world, night and day were one. Loud music was always blaring, the phones were always ringing, there was always food cooking, and people talking at each other in wild soliloquies.

We could not live with our failures and our doubts. So we turned up the music, turned on the booze and drugs, deceiving ourselves that in so doing we were creating another and better world. But it was a world that lacked all meaning. You must have meaning to live, and meaning comes only from long and honest struggle of the soul.

I made a paper airplane of my youthful heart. Its innocence burned in the fires of violence. But my heart never forgot its first innocence and hunger for beauty.

Cry out when the heart yearns to do so, young poet, and love your loneliness. Trust in the wisdom not accessible to reason. Let nothing be more important to you than the process of the poem. Read the poets; and eschew political theories, religious systems. Let poetry be your open space that you traverse with courage. Be true to your calling. Then may your words touch the multitudes, as a mother's kiss falls on the face of a dreaming child.

But advice, all advice, is like stale meat turning bad. I like my meals freshly cooked, by my own flame. So here I am, simply standing next to you, side by side, sharing with you some things that have inspired me to dance and forget myself in song. For all that, I still stumble like a fool, trying to make sense of my life.

To the poet has been given the power to conjure up winter in midsummer, if his heart so desires. He can sing the most hidden secrets of the heart. And these are gifts from God, before whom I lay prone, my face to the earth, in thanksgiving.

I have been a convict, an addict to booze and drugs; and the lover of life and juggler of words I am still. Here, in the park, see the man selling ice cream, the balloon man. Over there people are sitting on the grass. Two little girls screech with happiness at the pigeons following them. The church bells greet the sauntering crowds in their Sunday best. Upstairs, in a room off the common square, a man rises and pukes his guts into the toilet, the bitterness of last night's whiskey stings his chapped lips. Next door a man covers a woman, their hastily shed clothing mixed together on the floor. They whisper and sigh, grunt, and gyrate into each other as the sun illumines the floating dust motes that drift through the window.

I have given myself a lot of bad advice, but things are getting better. I don't hurt myself as much as I used to. Now, when I dive into an image of life, into the glistening metaphor, into the water, I don't crack my head as often. I believe that the water is deeper than I can see. I can't see bottom and I never will, but sometimes I can touch it. Now when I write, it's like the first time I felt my fingertips touch the bottom of a swimming pool. There was triumph in that, bravery and accomplishment. I don't come up bleeding anymore.

My life is a musical score, and each dawn I wake to play my trumpet notes to the new day, a new page turned. I step out among the trees like a child who has wandered far from his parents, into a forest. I don't understand why certain leaves are turning gray. I want to be with that tree and follow it to a place it knows, to the source of life, where one can be what he dreams, through the faith of the poem.

IV
Chicanismo:
Destiny and
Destinations

A View from the Other Side

No one knows how many Chicanos there are in this country. We are everywhere, in the millions, from New York to Califas, Alaska to Tejas, and, more than anywhere, in the Southwest. Our *mestizaje* defies all categories.

Some people arrogantly believe they retain the right to reject or legitimize our culture. They are wrong.

In the sixties we broke rank and allowed ourselves our difference, identified ourselves as Chicanos and discovered our uniqueness—painfully, courageously. We found our lineage in Mayan poets and Aztec warriors, Spanish kings, Mexican sheepherders, and farmers and ranchers along the Río Abajo, Nuevo Méjico.

Now there is a corporate effort to market us, but the questions of would-be employers barely conceal their still-surviving bigotry, that to them we are still a threat, can't be trusted, don't know enough, and that they are doing us a favor just to talk to us. Racism dies hard. The corporate and bureaucratic kennel-bosses who train employees to howl and bay and jump and wag their tails find that Chicanos won't jump through their hoops without a fight. We have lived on society's margins for five hundred years and freedom is in our blood.

In the textbooks of kindergarten to university, Anglo voices project an image of us that reflects little of the truth of our culture. In their version, we are fish-hatchery minnows spawned in Spain or Mexico or Latin America. They say we are meek, humble, self-effacing, willing to work for peon wages, yearning to be counterfeit Anglos, moths to the master's flame. I blow out that flame.

This winter morning on the farm, water, sky, earth, bare trees, and gray landscape haunt me with their bleakness; their grim resistance gives me a spectral inspiration. They whisper to my spirit that I am as old as they are on this land, and I need not suppress who I am, nor do I need permission to speak out.

Once I tried to be a *gavacho*, because the pain of being different was too great. Teachers rejected my Chicano identity, told me my culture came to nothing more than exotic decorations for the lives of the rich: feathers, drums, carvings, poems, songs, *santos*, dances, lapidary work were but antique stuffs for concert halls and museums, and it was time to forget, to assimilate.

Heady with the American myth of rugged individualism, I left the barrio to work as a laborer in Santa Fe. I was going to be as blue-eyed and blond-haired an American as anyone. Most of the Chicanos who had lived around the plaza were being pushed to the margins of town to make room for privileged Anglos whose jeweled parakeets cost more than Chicanos earned in a week, who drove their Mercedes and Jaguars to the construction sites where I worked and pointed their gold-tipped canes at the fields they wanted to buy. After a day's work building their pretentious playlands, I would climb the bulldozed mounds of dirt that separated rich from poor and make my way back to the barrio.

The bosses in their leather jackets and bomber pilot shades promised me, with hearty paternal backslaps, that one day I wouldn't be shoveling dirt, but counting money like the white folks. I noticed something strange: on the one hand, my people and our authentic culture were ridiculed; and, on the other, there was an approved, sanitized Anglo version, extracted from our art, of who we were and what we had done. Young white girls wore dresses like my grandmother's and raved about Spanish romanticism. White kids worked next to me in the trenches to get to know the Chicanos.

I was confused. I wanted to be a shiny generic commodity, a marketable Hispanic, packaged for the highest bidder. I was sick of the life of a straw-stuffed effigy, a baggage-carrying illiterate, of going to sleep at night hearing the feeble coughing of babies and grownups with the pulmonary illnesses of malnutrition and poverty. I wanted cozy comfort, security, a warm house, life insurance and medical coverage, fine clothes and a nice car, a good education. I wanted what they had.

I couldn't understand why these kids wanted to be like me when I was trying to be like them. Their lives were the fulfilled wish list of a favored child at Christmas. They admired my *chuco* baggies and ink-penned handkerchief, my straw hat and khaki shirt, and soon they were wearing to social engagements what I was wearing to work. It made no sense that my father's secondhand forties suit coat, that I wore because I couldn't afford better, was the featured *nouveau chic* in the plaza shop windows.

I went to work every morning with a gold-plated smile. But nothing changed, except that I was worked harder and paid less. After the summer, my Anglo workmates would go off to school or to dad's corporation. I didn't have those kind of nets in my life. You quit a job or got fired; you fell, and there was no dad or uncle to finance your failure. When an Anglo kid who had worked half as long as I got a raise and I didn't, I protested. I was fired.

With a sense of doom, knowing I was never to be *gavacho*, I went back to the barrio to take up my real life where I had left it. Instead of roasting chestnuts over a log fire, I warmed myself around a bonfire with Alfonso, whose hands and cheeks were numb from stringing fence around rich folks' houses—not fences where people met to exchange news, but fences that kept them apart.

Why couldn't I be successful being who I am—being

myself? Assimilation is a false apple whose red washes away in the rain. In the barrio, an apple is still an apple. Friends of mine in the barrio rebuked me for carrying on like a *gavacho*, they accused me of betraying *la gente*. I had violated a sacred covenant of *la raza*—that we must stick together and help each other, and remember who we are.

We are the weave of two rivers joined to create the braided cord of *chicanismo*. We are the blinding edge of light radiating behind the eclipse. We are the fresh hard bark on the tree that has grown from hundreds of generations at the core and our branches go out into both worlds, the indigenous and the European. Yet our homeland is under us. We stand on it, till it, harvest from it, tend its irrigation ditches. Our roots go deep, fusing with cataclysmic time when continental combustions fountained out fiery lava to form the earth. My memories are Aztlán torches that still flicker through all the stormy onslaughts of the invading occupiers of my land, still burn with their glowing earth connection.

Most of the Chicanos I know are earthbound and peaceful people, reaping a spiritual sustenance from their relationships with Mother Earth and *indio* Grandfather. But the wounds of greed score our lands. Our mothers were raped, our warriors were cut down by government-sanctioned bullets, hung from trees by vigilantes, thrown into prisons. But we endured.

There was a song my grandmother sang to me during hard times. The song was an *alabado*. When the wind struck up, fiercely ripping off tin roofs and toppling sheds, cracking boughs and blistering the air with dust and tumbleweeds, my grandmother rocked me in her arms and sang to me this holy folk song. My ear pressed against her chest bones, that seemed to me more powerful than the tornado-strong winds blowing outside. Her song vibrating in her bones, to the rhythm of her red-drum heart—beating, beating, beating— assuaged my terror, protected me from all the evil spirits flying in the air.

The recollection of her humming voice is one tentative branch-tip of my experience I shake seeds from, that they may fall on the fertile ground of my children's hearts. May these seeds grow strong.

Still, with the world so set on denying my culture, I am full of insecurities and my life is replete with contradictions, plummeting to mercuric chills and flaring to comet flights. I invite all possibilities of being as long as they don't oppress me. I affirm the right of my people to determine their destiny. I feel rage, hurt, pain, shame—and forgiveness, too. When I walk in the evening, a surge of euphoria from the earth fuses into my heels and hands, into my thoughts—a light fizz of energy. The delight of being here! Oppressors step aside to the banks of the road, because I am coming through.

Q-Vo*

Not long ago I received a letter from a Los Angeles watchdog committee concerned about the image of Chicanos and Latinos as portrayed in cinema. Part of a screenplay I have written, *Blood In . . . Blood Out* (working title), is set in a prison. This organization questioned the very subject of my script, saying that I should portray Chicanos in a more positive light. Their comments brought back many painful personal memories, and I find my answer to them in this present and that past.

When I was a kid growing up in the orphanage, I remember how I longed to learn to play the piano. Music and song always lifted me out of myself into rebellious reveries of enchantment. In the choir, when I opened my mouth to sing, my love for God and the angels came barreling out, and for all the orphans and everyone living on this earth. My throat muscles expanded and strained at the notes, my lungs pained with pure pleasure. When I sang, it seemed as if I were really talking to God and touching His ear with my small insignificant voice and my plea for a better world, and singing for His divine mercy.

But early on I noticed that my voice was not reaching Him. When it came time to choose those boys who would

*A phonetic representation of the Mexican and Chicano greeting "¿Qué hubo?" or "¿Quibo?": "What's happening?," " What's up?".

be taught to play, I pushed and shoved to the front of the line, squirming and biting my nails with anticipation. I knew I would be chosen. But they picked two other kids, Ricardo and Johnny, instead. I was told, with brutal indifference, that the piano was not for me.

Why them and not me? They were cleaner, neater, and better behaved. They combed their hair, and did their chores with prompt obedience. Did they have the gift of music, the love for it? The nuns didn't care about that, maybe they never even thought of it. But they had the right look and demeanor for the nuns to show off to the visitors who would come to recitals. They could be counted on to conduct themselves appropriately for these social gatherings.

Waiting for my name to be called, I saw myself flailing at the piano keys like a bronco-buster holding the reins of a wild mustang and never letting go, mastering its power. I had all this energy in me, telling me what I knew I could do with music, bending the notes to my passion and vision to make them express my sheer insane love of life.

With hindsight, I think the nuns knew it too, and this is just what they feared. They wanted to hear the Mass music politely played as the priest lifted the chalice, and not some ecstatic version of rock'n'roll. If they had let me loose, the notes would have triggered in me a desire to go farther, higher, to plunge into the unknown—the way it can happen when you put two notes together, and then another two. . . .

But, for all my desire, somewhere in me there lurked the suspicion that I did not deserve this chance, that I was not good enough to be chosen. The judgment of the adults had ripped through my aspirations like a dagger ripping through silk.

At the orphanage, the good boys got the attention and came out on top. My friends and I were river rats, swimming upstream in muddy ditches, seven-year-old *vatos* puffing on homemades—dried elm leaves wrapped in strips of comic papers. We laughed without reserve, careening down the slides and swinging from the monkey bars. Our clothes were worn to shreds from our wild acrobatics. We carried life in our pants cuffs and pockets—leaves and sand, twigs and pebbles, marbles and bits of string, broken buttons and old Indian-head pennies. Like scruffy dogs, we were always burying things and digging them up, things of value to no one else but to which we attached a mystical importance, creating with them imagined and magical worlds.

Early on I recognized that the outside world was fueled on hypocrisy. When visitors came to the orphanage, the nuns showed them a cookie cut-out version of Bing Crosby's *Going My Way*, with angelic kiddies clinging to Father's black-robed graces, and nuns that were saccharine Ingrid Bergmans, full of humility and religious fervor.

But that's not the way it was. Life, and my life there, was very different—as a novel I'm writing will show. I could never become a dancing bear for the ringmaster's whip. I was not the submissive little brown Indian-Chicano, fanning Master White Man and singing a Southwest version of *Hiawatha*. Tonto and Kimosabe was not a game I could play.

It didn't get any better out in society, in junior high. That world belonged to the gringos, to the flag raisers and national anthem singers. The standards there were the same. Our teachers, male and female, were nuns without habits or vows, bent on molding little conformists to the mainstream norm.

But it wasn't only the Anglos who kept us down. Most of the Hispanics we knew disapproved of us too, and tried to make us deny our culture and emulate white society. But that wasn't who we were, and we knew it.

When one of my books, *Martín & Meditations on the South Valley*, was published, several Hispanic scholars decried the honesty of my depiction of Hispanic life. They said, in effect, that Hispanic writers should present a purely positive image of our people. According to their view, Chicanos never have betrayed each other, we never have fought each other, never sold out; nor have we ever experienced poverty or suffering, wept, made mistakes. I never responded to these absurdities: such narrowness and stupidity is its own curse. My answer is to go on telling the truth—the whole truth—leaving these misguided critics to their illusions.

Because I am a Chicano, it does not mean that I am immune from the flaws and the sufferings that make all of us human; and, first and last, I am a human being. But I am Chicano through the values and the spirit passed on to me by my people and through my own personal experience. Some people, like these critics, take the energy from the loins, that incredible lust of love, and transfer it into their brains, until they forget how to make love. They take the energy, the life-force, from their heart and cram it into their brains until they are bereft of passion in the heart and lust in the loins, and in this they take pride. And from this abortion their passionless and dreamless analysis is born.

In prison, when I wrote to the G.I. Forum asking for books, they never replied. I wrote to university departments of Chicano Studies—no response. It was the same with LULAC* and other organizations I appealed to, to help me educate myself. All of them obliquely referred to my "predicament" as not being pertinent to their cause. I was an embarrassment because I didn't fit into their concept of Chicano reality.

Who gave me the encouragement to learn to read and to write? It came from the Chicano *vatos* in prison who gave me books and pencils. And it came from friends and lovers, and from the barrio activists who visited us in prison. They were the ones who raged to the judges about our mistreatment, who won the victories against those who would flagrantly abuse our civil and human rights. They were the spiritual warriors who fought for us loyally, shoulder to shoulder. My

---

*League of United Latin American Citizens

poems sing for them, and for the oppressed on both sides of the prison bars.

Years later, I came out of prison with fifty dollars in my pocket and no trust for anyone. No job was waiting for me. I was terrified. Society had branded me, as it brands every ex-con, convinced that we want only to maim and destroy. What I wanted was simply to get my life together, but I didn't know how. I wanted to be loved and to love. I wanted what everyone wants—a happy and meaningful life—and I was willing to work for it, to do almost anything to get it, to be accepted.

But it didn't happen, not for a long time. In truth, the "vengeance" of the ex-con is nothing to the viciousness shown to him by mainstream society, through the perpetuation of an image of us as less than human, and therefore irredeemable.

Ten years after my release, when, as an invited guest, I toured universities in Arizona reading my poetry, I asked my wife to drive me to one of the prisons where I had been held. I thought I was strong enough to go back, but when we drove into the parking lot I saw a guard leaving at the end of his shift, the same guard who used to come into my cell with other guards to torment me. All the anguish I had buried for so many years suddenly erupted, and I started to shake. I bent low in my seat, gagging and vomiting, weeping uncontrollably, and I told my wife to drive away fast. Memories of the pain and torture I had endured in prison came flooding back to overwhelm me. I had gone there looking for an answer, but there was no answer, only silence.

I made a promise then, for all the *vatos* I left behind the prisons bars, not to forget them, to write honestly about what we had endured. This is what I have tried to do in my film script *Blood In . . . Blood Out*. Yes, Chicanos and blacks do fight in prison. Yes, blacks and whites do kill each other in prison. Yes, there is violence in the script I have written. Yes, my critics, who would deny the full truth of our reality and our experience, some of us have been locked away in prisons. And, yes, in this film I have cried out my rage, and nakedly shown the pain and abuse of life behind bars. All of this is an authentic part of our reality, and to deny it is to make us less than what we are.

I write to reveal all the treasures of Chicano experience, all that I have learned about life through our heritage, with nothing left out, of the suffering and the joy, because *all* of it has made us who we are. I believe that we will never overcome our obstacles unless we tell the whole truth, and in everything I write this is what I strive to do.

And, in truth, my film is about much more than the brutality of prison life. It is about kids trying to find out who they are, about kids growing into men faced with hard choices, and about living with, or dying from, the consequences of those choices. *Blood In . . . Blood Out* does not serve any political camp, nor paint barrio life as a paradise. But it reflects my experience and my reality in all their complexity.

Granted, some aspects of this reality into which I invite you demand, in part, a willingness to journey into the dark side of life, into those obscure places in the human soul that strike fear when we encounter them in ourselves and in others. Yet I believe there are jewels to be discovered in the darkness: jewels that can shed light on our lives, illuminations.

On Ash Wednesday our foreheads are smudged with ash to remind us that we are imperfect and mortal. It is a reminder of the imperfection or wound we carry from birth, and of how sweet and fleeting life is; a reminder that in our relationships to each other we should conduct ourselves with humility and decency.

When we do not acknowledge the wound, when we do not accept it, or refuse to hear those who remind us of our imperfection, when we conceal it from ourselves and from others, we begin to believe our wound does not exist. We become arrogant, believing we are as gods who can impose our will upon others, denying any vision of reality but our own.

Where I come from, the white-male-run government robs us of our land, and the schools forbid us to speak our native language and honor our culture. Where I come from, infants are born diseased and without limbs. Where I come from, the air is thick with pollutants, the fields are gangrenous with pesticides. Where I come from, old people eat from trash cans and freeze to death in the doorways where they sleep. Where I come from, there are fathers who sexually abuse their daughters, maiming them for life, mothers who are crackheads, and neighborhoods run by gangsters. Where I come from, there is violence and racial conflict and corruption. And yet, miraculously, there is sweetness and beauty there, too.

When I am at a backyard party with my friends, listening to Chicano music, and I see all these brown faces, young and old, spiritual euphoria permeates my being. My life becomes a celebration in honor of my people. They are a people who have suffered and worked and endured; whose stubborn reverence and love for life we call *corazón*. Perhaps this is why I write, to pay homage to my people and their ways.

Writing is my way of hearing and talking to God, of relinquishing my human faculties to the power that springs from human joy and suffering. I write suspended in hummingbird flight and dance with the darkness. I fall into a semi-consciousness in which my gut speaks to me and my blood cries out. I walk through fire. I hurt all over.

The writer must be free to go crazy, whether with ecstasy or pain, to explode the indifference of a world that accepts that 'home' for some families is a nest of cardboard boxes, that accepts such abominations. The writer must be free to delve into the offensive and the vile, to rut in the mud as in the flowers, and to challenge with the truth of his vision and experience the keepers of the lie and the wielders of oppression, no matter where they are found.

This is why I will not refrain from telling you that it was Hispanic cops who handcuffed me and beat me unconscious in the basement of the Albuquerque County Jail one Valentine's Day, a beating of such brutality that for weeks after I was confined to a hospital. And why? For refusing to be patted down and fingerprinted, for refusing to be humiliated and treated like an animal. In a jail where the cons were ninety-nine percent Chicano, Chicano cops beat me with murderous force, secure in the knowledge that no one would hold them accountable.

When I tell these stories—true stories—Chicanos and others who are lucky enough to have the resources to distance themselves from such experiences may be disturbed. Such incidents are upsetting to hear about. But these things happen every day in hundreds of jails, and in the barrios from New York to Los Angeles.

In my film script, the young street-gang members are not simply antisocial monsters, but victims too. Why are these youths so unthinkingly condemned when so many other human groups, respected organizations fat with power, are essentially, with the window dressing stripped away, nothing but gangs: corporate enforcers of their views, conscienceless wielders of power?

When I write about barrio life, I do not cloak its darker aspects in shame and silence, because to bring them into the open is to reveal essential human impulses, distorted by pain and suffering, from which they are born. I reap the neglected harvests of our hearts, the pain, the ugliness and the beauty that make us human, as lovely and noble as any creatures on earth.

And I do not conceal my bitterness. In my life in prison and on the street, my soul screamed for someone to help, to tell the world what was happening to me. The experience of writing a film script about that time has reawakened my awareness of the killing silence imposed on the imprisoned and on the youthful condemned, and of how silence endangers the soul of those who have the power to speak.

And so I speak out. I want all of us—from grade school

Chicano and Chicana to grandmother and grandfather—and all of you, to know what happens to those of us who are forced to lived on the margins of society. Prison did not rehabilitate me. Love for my people did, love for my family. The people who cared for me and loved me are the ones who have helped me heal the damage done to me in prison.

This is an exciting time for our Chicano community. After being crushed by centuries of contempt, we are finally getting to our feet and creating for ourselves opportunities for a better life. Among ourselves and in mainstream society, there is a growing recognition of our potential political and economic power. We no longer are tempted to deny the riches of our language, our arts and our culture. Nor should we deny the full spectrum of our experience, our light and our dark— both are precious, because we lived them. This is no time for factionalism and quarreling among ourselves. Let us, as brothers and sisters, support each other now in a full exploration of the Chicano experience which will deepen the understanding of ourselves and of our reality in the broader community.

It is true, historically, that the mainstream media has perpetuated an image of our people as prone to crime, to drug addiction. Dark skins seem to signify dark deeds. Their best-intentioned efforts have produced little more than patronizing caricatures. It also has been true that mainstream accounts of the meeting of two cultures, the European and the Indio, were made into quaint fairytale versions of this chapter in American history. But recently the truth has begun to emerge, revelations of a people robbed and insulted and murdered, forced to leave their ancestral lands and to become displaced in time and history.

For centuries, fear held dominion in the hearts of my people. But now we have begun to speak out, where before we locked away in silence the truth we knew.

My film, *Blood In . . . Blood Out*, has a message. It is

that no one has the right to oppress another, to so damage him that he is prevented from living life to the fullest. No one has the right to terrorize another human being, to break his spirit, to debase him and strip him of hope and dignity.

I had such a good feeling the other day, playing miniature golf with my two sons. Across the street was the high school I was expelled from after only a few weeks as a student there. The principal, in his parting speech, assured me that I was no good and would never amount to anything. I remember keenly, as if it were yesterday, my humiliation and anger.

But now, looking over at that building as I horsed around with my two beautiful boys, my life was not so bad. And I smiled and gave thanks to the powers of creation for letting me live to reach this moment: to enjoy the love of my wife and my sons and my friends, and for the gift of writing.

Who am I to tell others what they should see or hear? My imperatives are for myself alone: to labor to see more light in the darkness, to become a better father to my sons, to be a more acute and loving observer of my fellow human beings. I am, before anything else, a poet; and all my forty years until now have been an apprenticeship to write one good poem, to know one solid truth, to be able to love, and to be worthy of receiving love. And to remain true to my reality, that in so doing I may honor my people and pay full homage to their spirit.

¿De Quiéncentennial?
Puro Pedo . . .*

Corporations and government agencies in North America and Europe are preparing Columbus's anniversary. It will be five hundred years since his arrival in America in 1492. The event will be celebrated with Rose Garden toddy-tippling, military hoorays, patriotic pep talks. Pilgrim artifacts will be on display in shop windows, and the media moguls are sure to be endorsing the European version of history with books and movies. The streets will hemorrhage with parades of patriotic hysteria, showboating a few assimilated Indians on floats, radiating the servility of the conquered; and arrogant Spanish aristocrats will nod to the giddy crowds hoisting flags and banners that proclaim the five-hundredth birthday of this continent's discovery.

In the French Quarter recently, the locals staged a little parade in which they playfully mocked those public dignitaries who insult our intelligence. One contingent marched by holding up a large placard—GENITALIA OF THE RICH AND FAMOUS—behind which Margaret Thatcher's vagina crumpled over the head of a midget and Reagan's penis battled with Bush's. The placard of the next group of frolicking minstrels, SAVINGS & LOAN SCANDAL, portrayed a

---

*This title incorporates a bilingual pun, "¿de quién?" meaning "whose": Whose quincentennial is it anyway? [Not *mine*, being implied.] It's a crock . . .

taxpayer bending over with his pants down and a huge penis about to penetrate into the taxpayer's ass. Musicians of all ages cavorted and pranced, blowing their saxophones and trumpets and banging their drums, laughing away our American blues.

Contrast this parade with the one that was staged for the pope's visit to America, when police dragnets swept up all evidence of poverty and hopelessness in our cities. We showed him the sanitized America of the commercials, where every American brushes his teeth after every meal, an anesthetized America, which the upcoming celebrations, too, will no doubt proclaim as heavenly truth.

I have no real sense of participation in the national identity of this country, no sense that I am represented. No statesman or public figure ever has spoken effectively on my behalf. I learned about American justice when I was sixteen, chained to a pillar in the basement of the county jail, and in courts where rich kids got off free on the same charges for which brown brothers and sisters are doing time. My sense of that justice is sharpened on train rides, when immigration officers sweeping through ask me for my I.D.

Recently I was a member of a panel that met to discuss funding of the arts in the barrio. The audience was composed mostly of Anglo administrators and directors of cultural programs in the cities and towns of New Mexico. The panel members were Native Americans, Chicanos and blacks, of the tame variety. They were grateful for the opportunity to come before us, they said, to report how well things were going in their respective quarters. When it came my turn to speak, this cooing of doves turned into a backyard cockfight. In spite of what everyone seemed to be saying, all was not well, I said. I told them that in the hard-pressed lives of barrio artists, living hand to mouth, there isn't a lot of time for learning about filling in grant applications; in the little boxes that designate ethnicity, there isn't even a category for Chicanos.

One Anglo woman stood up to protest, saying how all the Indians and Spanish and Anglos got along so well in Taos, how they meditated together and shared company and nodded to each other, and met at the community center to play music and to dance. I wanted to ask her how much stolen land the Anglos had given back to the Taos *indios*, who had fought for this in the courts for decades. If you come into a place and can take all the land with impunity, it's easy to smile at your victims. For those marauders, it was a child's candy-shop fantasy.

Let me hear the whole truth about this country's history. The Chicano experience permeates every thread of this country's historical fabric. But countless among us have had to spend our strength addressing wrongs committed against us along the United States–Mexican border, in factories, on school boards, in migrant workers' camps, and in prisons, universities, barrios, and rural villages. Some day we all will come together in our millions, from east, west, north, and south, from hundreds of barrio tribes, to proclaim our truth. But, until then, businessmen will go on reaping windfall revenues from the injustices done to us, politicians will continue to profit from the lies they tell about us, and the land developers and those who run the banks, schools and corporations will continue to feast on the misery and disenfranchisement of our people.

I have many Anglo friends whom I consider family. They have strong opinions and compassionate hearts, they have worked all their lives, they practice a healthy sense of fair play. I speak now of the others, those who hold power and abuse it, dispensing unjust laws, selecting the books of half-truths we read in our schools, determining whose neighborhoods and roads will be improved and whose will be neglected: those who wield disproportionate power by manipulation and corruption. The Quincentennial will reflect their vision of America, not mine. They command the TV stations and the motion picture industry, the publishing houses and the advertising media. Their interests make the news of the world.

I am certain that the Quincentennial celebrations will not acknowledge the fact that I, as a Chicano, am persecuted judicially and economically, that I live in an occupied territory. Nor that I am deprived of my civil rights because I speak a language different from that of mainstream America, and am subtly oppressed from birth to death because of my heritage. I must speak for the many whose voices will not be heard in the official Quincentennial clamor, above the riot of mindless celebrations, moneymaking and electioneering.

I insist that my culture and heritage be reflected to the world in a way that makes my children proud of who they are and of their father who is part of the American mosaic. Chicanos have built America's railroads, bridges and roads, schools and cathedrals, written her novels and poems, made songs and dances, and died in American wars. Yet, these contributions are ignored, and to many we are invisible.

But we are a living presence, here in the millions, right before your eyes. Chicano language, that you cannot hear, has conveyed our most intimate loves and pains for five hundred years. Chicano culture, a veil over the jade mask of our Mayan heart, merges the present with the primordial past in our experience. Our language, which I have inherited, is a symphony of rebellion against invaders, and love of earth. In my Chicano blood many tributaries meet—the blood of silver-mine Mexican-Indian slaves, of Mexican sheepherders and Apache warriors, of French trappers and Spanish conquistadors.

By ignoring our culture, America can disclaim the guilt of the ruthless neglect of our people. But we cherish our unassimilated identity. The oral tradition of *la raza* lives. We belong to the land we live on and will always belong. We take our spiritual power from Mother Earth to endure and our spiritual covenant has not been broken.

The bent backbones of field workers are the vertebrae of our harrowed fields. The red of our earth is made from the blood of the countless victims of the vigilantes, colonial missionaries, and frontiersmen, those who were mercilessly slaughtered because they refused to be driven off their ancestral lands.

But we are still here. On the margins of society you will find us. And you will find us also in our poetry and theater, in our dance and music, and in the carvings and paintings that reflect our deep roots. As a poet, I integrate through my art the paradoxes of my Spanish and Indian heritages. Through art I question the legitimacy of institutions that exclude us. Through art I assert myself against racism and injustice, and proclaim with my people the melting of their chains in the fire of a vision for a better life. I represent myself and I create myself. The power usurped from me to decide my affairs I take back to myself. This is my celebration.

I am the rebellious wolf cub, who has wept between my grandmother-wolf's gnarled paws, and laughed and howled with her under the moon on the mesa. Hair grows from her hundred-year-old face, her pad-feet prowl the night in the llano. *She is the oldest wolf-woman of our family and I am the youngest wolf, who hunts in the darkness of spirit regions and licks the hairy belly of earth. The moon is a lemon grove I travel in. She has stared at me with white eyes, cataract-glacier eyes, silvery deep mirrors, and made me grieve my insensitivity.*

I am wolf-man. I belong to the wolf-woman who bore five sons and six daughters. Some, while she worked in the field, she gave birth to on the dirt, under a tree; others she gave birth to on a wagon, lying on her back in hay; others she gave birth to in a barn. And the blood of the young wolves who died at birth in her hard labor my soul licks. One arm I raise in love for life while my other hand scratches at the dirt, and I bare my fangs, growling at our travails.

I prowl the margins of society, for if I go too near they will kill me. So I hug the shadows, traveling by night, and snatch sleep snuggled with my children in stony caves and arroyos. *When*

I leave cover, I sniff the ground and air for signs of luck. I am wolf-poet, traveling in the swirling snow of the imagination, writing down mystic metaphors from the mad landscapes of my heart.

The Quincentennial will celebrate the past: the brutal subjugation of a continent, the destruction of its natural resources, the raping of indigenous cultures. But our culture is now, and constantly changing through our spiritual odyssey. Its emptying center, open for new meanings, awaits the quiet passage of the spirit that speaks in our arts.

Chicano culture is young, vibrant, ever-reaching and risking, and each new step we take renews our sense of who we are. I am constantly discovering who I am, how my Spanish and Indian heritages speak to each other of anger, forgiveness, and love, creating a third voice, the Chicano voice.

The collapse of borders between *indio* and Spanish created an intermarriage of tribes, an exchange not only of goods but of cultural wisdom. Wool was traded for leather, turquoise for obsidian, silver for gold, tortillas for *piñones, vigas* for adobe bricks, la Virgen de Guadalupe for Tonantzín, farming methods for hunting skills, the magic of herbs for the magic of animal parts, lyrics of religious songs for the chants of tribal ceremonies. From the integration of these vital exchanges the Chicano culture was born.

Finding no understanding of *mestizaje* experience in the accepted texts, I was compelled to create my own synthesis, choosing from the plurality of my past, rejecting the European fragments that told so little of our story. Spain has a very beautiful culture and there are aspects of it in my blood; some of Spain's history is appalling. What I find most essential to my growth as a human being, I have chosen from the *indio* and Chicano cultures. There also is French blood in me, and in that culture's poetry, also, I have found kinship.

Recently I was a member of another panel in which the daughters of Martin Luther King and Malcolm X also were participants. After the discussion we took questions from an audience of five thousand high school kids. Five long queues extended in front of our five microphones. I was happy to see so many black youths lining up to ask questions, even though they were mostly interested in what it feels like to be a 'star', and there were few serious questions about Malcolm's or Dr. King's visions for a better country. However, what truly saddened me was that there was not a single Chicano youth among the questioners. They outnumbered the blacks and whites by at least thirty-to-one, but not a single Chicano stood up to ask a question.

Why do we maintain this public silence? In my personal life, everywhere I turn I am surrounded with the lively words and vibrant voices of my people, laughing and telling stories, asking questions. We must break out of our silence before outsiders and tell them what we think. I love Muhammad Ali for telling the world what he thought during the heyday of his boxing career.

We must make that ancient drum beat again for us, and let our guitar strings and voices resound with our passion, with songs of our love and rage. We must leap into the Quincentennial arena like jaguars. We must let our dreams enflame the hickory wood of history to create our own light, a light that will blend with the undying pyres of poets who have died because they told the truth.

Out of our dark silence, let us bring up the dark jewels of a new vision for ourselves, a shining *chicanismo* that expresses our spirit, our alliance of indigenous peoples. Let us awaken in ourselves and in each other a deep pride for having survived the brutality of oppression.

Somehow, we survived our oppressors. And survived the struggles among ourselves—the drunken brawls in which we 'proved' ourselves by destroying ourselves and each other—survived our rage against the *gavachos*, and our loneliness when we left the barrio in search of new ways to live.

Sometimes we closed our eyes with pain. We wept because

we could not endure the shame of being taught to hate ourselves, and could not withstand the tragedy of our lives. And when we came together for fiestas or *resolanas*, sometimes the beauty was too much for us. We wept because our brothers were drunks and our sisters rejected us, because our families fell apart in hopelessness. We fought each other, we accused and betrayed each other, reviled those who tried to escape from the barrio, raged at those who stayed behind, and cursed at those who took on Anglo ways. And some of us closed our eyes to life and died from overdoses, or sacrificed ourselves in war, because the suffering at home was too great and the pain in the heart too intense.

We lost control of our lives. We labored at lackey chores and our women screamed that we were not men. The world told us that we were not men, that we were unworthy of respect, and our tragedy was that we half believed it. We should have filled the streets with the clamor of our protest, but we remained silent, our culture fugitive and hidden.

I smell in my children's skin the earth, and sense in their hearts how truth does not die, how they flash with serpent's-tongue awareness of our people. And their days are hawk-feathered, spread out in joy for life, folded in respect for death. Now, during the Quincentennial and after, let our voices be heard, and let our children and the whole world hear at last what is in our hearts.

L.A., Ése . . . *

The plane took off from the International Airport in Albuquerque, New Mexico. Looking out the window at the gray landscape below, I could see my small farm at Black Mesa, nestled under trees like a wren's adobe nest. The Río Grande switched back and forth, symbol of Quetzalcoátl, God of Dawn. Every spring my children and I enter the snake's mouth for our blessings. I wade out, water lapping around my thighs, one child on my shoulder and the other holding my hand, and we make our pilgrimage to a sand bar island where we play in the mud and splash in the ankle-high water.

In earlier years, friends and I would park under the cottonwood trees there, to smoke joints, drink beer and listen to Chicano music. The way an Aztec high priest walked a brave warrior up the pyramid temple steps to sacrifice his heart to the sun is the way I come to the landscape of New Mexico. It takes my soul and smolders it off the slab rock of canyons, rinses it in the ditch waters, dries it in the prairie. My heart breathes in the fragrance of red corn and pinto beans and green chiles. When I visit a friend's house, where the porch is piled high with gunnysacks of red corn, and in the kitchen pinto beans steam and green chile sizzles in an iron fry pan, I am strengthened and familiar with my heart. I know what I want in life, what I want to say and how I want to live.

---

*L.A., dude . . .

Somehow, I am always leaving New Mexico, maybe because my people from way back have been wandering sheepherders and prairie riders, following the fertile season. But in my blood is the blue sky and clear light, the rocks and fields, the chile and beans and tortillas of Nuevo Méjico. These are my blessings. When I die, fill my mouth with yellow corn and my palms with pinto beans to take with me as gifts into the other world.

I was sixteen when I first left New Mexico, headed for San Diego. My life had fallen apart like a wet paper bag. Even though it held all the provisions for happiness, it tore, and my dreams and hopes lay scattered all around me. I had made a discovery that stunned me, ending a youthful romance that had lasted five years.

My girlfriend had phoned to ask me to meet her at her apartment. When I opened the door, I saw her lying on the floor entangled in the embrace of several women, all of them naked. They looked up at me with liquid eyes and lazy smiles, as if to say, "Got you, bastard!" The images of those thighs and breasts and twining arms braided like a hangman's rope around my neck, and when my love looked up at me and caressed her sex, the trapdoor went out from under me. It was a bumper crop of female rage that year.

This was a woman at whose feet I had lain like a dog, who had ignored me and lied to me and insulted me. At the end, most of my days were spent alone even though we were still together. How many times had my fists beaten in rage against the stucco walls of her house? How many times had I waited on cold, snowy nights for her to come home? How many times had she whispered in my ear sweet lies and broken promises? How I adored her; shamed myself and humiliated myself to prove my love to her. It was a love affair of brutal deceit and crushing disappointment.

Late that night I found myself in a bar with a bottle of tequila in front of me and a pile of quarters for the jukebox. Tequila and song to numb poisonous love. After a while,

Rogina, one of the cocktail waitresses, came over and sat with me. When she told me about her boyfriend beating her, I suggested she move in with me for a time.

In those days, I had an old adobe hut on South Isleta, with a doorless outhouse that looked out on a cornfield. A ladder led up to the flat roof where we could lie and look at the stars, smoking weed, drinking wine, helping each other to drown the blues. Or we would lie in bed and listen to the wood crackling in the potbelly stove. Rogina was beautiful, but we never made love. After breaking up with my girlfriend, sex had as much appeal for me as a castor oil cocktail. We would go to bed naked, but all we did was talk, till we fell asleep—Joni Mitchell songs on the radio, a chill breeze crackling the corn leaves, and crows cawing by the river at dawn.

Rogina's hobbies were making candles and drinking 'boat', a cough medicine with a high percentage of alcohol. She spent most of her time by the wood stove, with her sand pile, wax, wicks and jars. I spent my time drugged, trying to dull the pain of rejection.

I was asleep one morning when a sharp click by my ear woke me. I opened my eyes and stared into the barrel of a .45.

Behind the gun was a black man shouting, "Wha' t' fuck you doing wid my bitch, muthafucka!"

Rogina woke up. She looked as terrified as I felt. "Clarence . . . he hasn't touched me . . . we haven't . . ."

"Shut yo' fucken trap bitch, I'll fucken pistol whip yo' ass!" In a face pocked with white battle scars, his left eyelid was twitching.

"Listen . . ." But I stopped, not knowing what to say.

He stared at us and then pulled off the blankets.

"You be sleeping naked and not fucken her . . . boo'shit." He cocked the hammer back.

"I haven't made love to her . . . ," I said, not caring if he shot me or not. That period in my life, I didn't care. I stared at him.

He stared back.

"You a funny muthafucka. . . ." Then to Rogina, "Bitch, dis man corncob you?"

"I told you . . . Clarence, he hasn't touched me."

Clarence smiled and slowly put away his gun.

"Well, I'll be a muthafucka . . . you impotent as a old hen. . . ." He chuckled and his eyelid quit twitching. "Alright, get yo' clothes on woman and git us some barbecue pork from Powdrell's down the road. Hear me, git on it, woman. . . ."

Rogina pulled on her jeans and shirt in a hurry and left us. Clarence and I sat down at the table by the wood stove and had coffee. He was intrigued by how a man gets impotent.

"I loved her," I began, "but it was all wrong, our relationship. I got stung. I tried to show her I loved her, but it was like trying to breathe under water. There was something missing, gone, something I forgot to learn. . . ."

"She a jaw-raw kooch-squatter. . . ," he said.

I laughed. The memory of her hurt.

"Gotta keep dem bitches on a choke chain." He set his .45 on the table. "Nice, huh?"

"Never owned one." I paused. "You should treat Rogina better, man, and quit beating on her. She's a stand-up woman." I told him that when she went with me to score some drugs she always held her own. She did what she had to do and gave me backup.

On one occasion we were drinking with friends in a bar and the bartender didn't bother to tell us he had closed up, or maybe he did but we were too drunk to notice. Anyway, the cops came and the four of us, three guys and Rogina, duked it out with them.

They handcuffed me and put me in the front seat and her in the back. I kicked the windshield out and the cop got on the radio to say he was bringing us in. When I kicked out his talkie-box, he pulled over and billy-clubbed the hell out of me. Rogina kicked at him, that long Rockette's leg of hers went up and her heel spike went right through his cheek.

After Rogina got back, the three of us sat around eating and talking about where to score some speed. Clarence had decided to let Rogina stay with me, because in my condition, he said, it was like putting a vegetarian in front of a plate of barbecued pork. So we lived together for a few more months and Clarence would drop by to take her out from time to time.

One day I told her I was leaving. I don't think I knew what I meant by that, nor did Rogina. She stood in the doorway, beautiful, and I was crazy. The sun was on her long red hair and pale skin and floral skirt. Her green eyes were saying good-bye. I backed my car slowly out of the yard, knowing only that I wanted to drive to get the discontentment out of my bones. I took nothing with me. It was as if I were going around the corner to pick up a loaf of bread. But I never returned, and I never saw Rogina again.

It was late March and the buds and leaves were coming out and the world seemed baby-fresh. I drove under a long tunnel of cottonwoods, the leaves flashing iridescent sparks that reflected off the shiny car trim; and I just wanted to keep the wind in my face, let it keep hitting my cheeks and whipping the tears off my eyelids. On my tongue was the black, crusty ash taste of sorrow.

I thought of the times I had caught my girlfriend kissing other men behind my back. She had problems with her father, but I didn't know how to help her. The remedy for everything was smoke a doobie, drink a lot, and fuck. Our fucking was mechanical, pure lust. Something in each of us opposed the other, preventing total surrender and abandon. After sex I felt like I had paid a bill, done my duty; and she looked as if she had suffered a grave internal injury.

One day an uncle of mine went out to empty the trash behind the house and vanished. Six years later he called from Las Vegas to say he was coming back. My aunt told me about it with a faint smile on her lips, as if she understood men. My cousin had two families, two wives living within three blocks of each other for ten years, until he told both families about each other. It seemed to me, in both cases, that no one had suffered an ungodly amount of pain. Such things run in the blood, I guess; because here I was doing the same kind of thing.

I needed some pocket change to get me wherever I was going. I had an old trailer in a trailer park that I hadn't paid the rent on for six months, so I seldom went there. The trailer was not worth much, but if I sold it that would cover the back rent and a bit more besides.

I made Mr. Martínez, the trailer park owner, an offer. He gave me a thousand, wiped the debt clean, and kept the trailer. He didn't seem too worried when I told him I had lost the title; he figured he could get another one. So we shook hands and I took off for one of the many mobile home sales companies that line East Central in Albuquerque. In the office of the sales manager, I pulled out my title and sold the trailer a second time for another thousand. Then I went to my sister's and told her that if she still wanted the rock table in the trailer, for a hundred bucks she could have it and the rest of the furniture too. Then I called a friend to tell him that if he picked up my old truck at the trailer park it was his.

My friend later told me, between fits of hysterical laughter, that when he went to pick up the truck Mr. Martínez and the mobile home sales manager and my sister were all there, arguing over the trailer and its contents. They were yelling their claims and counterclaims at about the same time that I was passing through Needles, California.

I drove as far as I could, to Ocean Park, and pulled in to look at the ocean. The surfers and beach poets, homosexuals and bikinied girls had a healthy orange juice glow, their cheeks sea-sprayed strawberries. I looked like a pothole in asphalt that jolts you when you run into it.

I came to California to bury my love for a woman. I took the dying starfish of my heart, touched its spiked and scaly skin, and threw it into the waves and walked away. I wanted to listen to sad stories about love told by old seamen fishing on the pier. The ocean is the dream mortuary, where so many dreams die. I sniffed the air, melancholy with loves that have perished.

Soon after I had sold my car for rent money, I met Marcos, a guy from Michigan who had a hot black Duster. We got into selling drugs, running the border and burning rubber from Mexico to L.A., buying and selling weed, and scoring PCP for servicemen trying to make it through basic training in San Diego. We ended up in the county jail doing six months for unpaid speeding tickets. Marcos's parents bailed him out but I did my time, got my new pedigree papers, a dog with a rap sheet who was let out of the pound early one morning to nose his way down alleys and growl his freedom in the labyrinth of L.A. streets.

Memories of my past continued to unwind as the pilot informed us we were coming into Los Angeles and the stewardess checked to make sure we were buckled up.

I looked out the porthole window and remembered myself, a teenage Chicano kid with balls so huge I was bowlegged at five, balls full of apocalypse emotion, aflame with love and bravado, grooving to the song "Me and Mrs. Jones," my life already a splintered bow pulled back to the breaking point, aiming its arrowhead heart into the sun, a kid singing what felt like his last cry of love for life.

Getting off the plane, full of feeling for the kid I had been, I sniffed that familiar tropical ocean breeze. There was a chauffeur holding up a card with my name on it.

"Mr. Baca?"

"Yes."

"Your bag, please follow me, the limo is below."

I was out here alone again, but this time I wasn't afraid, I was happy, delighted. I had survived the violence of my life to enjoy this moment. After fifteen years of earning nothing from my poetry, a fifteen-year workweek, it felt good to know I was going to get paid for this movie gig. I felt like the stag must feel his first spring, when buck fever swells his cock and he bellows for a doe. My antlers were ready for the challenge.

In my prison cell I had vowed that if the world did not let me in, someday I would welcome the world into my world. It was happening.

In the LAX lobby, where busy passengers pressed toward their gates, I wanted to leap up and yell my happiness to them and make my joy a communal dance: all of us dropping our suitcases, pausing for a moment from schedules and appointments, to just fucking dance.

Back in sunny California again, rolling along on worn heels that make me walk awkward, hair thinning to a balding monk's circle on the back of my head, I promised myself to get healthy—exercise, eat vitamins, stop smoking and drinking, join the YMCA, get into a spa. No more leafing bleary-eyed through my personal phone book to call friends at three in the morning; no more getting high on drugs and stopping at phone booths in New York or Philly, in the cold snow and whipping wind, calling appointments I'd missed because I was partying all night; no more trains and planes and cars and buses, and me bleakly staring out the windows wishing for a secure life someday, loving and being loved. . . .

But despite all these promises to myself, there comes a night when I laugh and laugh, a horrible, dangerous, on-the-brink-of-madness laughter, a deep gypsy laughter, a wildly dark laughter with no tomorrow; because nothing can shield me from the uppercut that life will always land cleanly on my chin from the blind side. I like to confront life, and I'll probably never change, but I'll keep trying.

I walked through LAX with all the past rushing in my veins. It was a rutting moment in time, when my sadness wanted to sing, to grunt love and penetrate the soundproof windows and walls of LAX with my semen, to pierce into people's innermost secrets with my heavenly howl of orgasm, humming my journey's madness like Sam Cooke's mellow gladness for nights lived, for lies whispered into his saxophone. Grateful for slaps in the face, for grief and forgiveness given and received; glad for the freeing of me, for still reaching out to trust, each time a little more, risking a little more, taking the extra inch forward that could mean destruction— but to do it, yeah, just do it, take the nectarine terror of life in my palm and squeeze it and let the juice run into the wound and burn with awakening pain of what it is to be honest and good and loving. Yes, heart of mine, you, Jimmy, with your thief laughter and heedless hunger to know life in a song of bursting light and fire, you, Jimmy, shy brown-eyed boy, weeping blackberry tears on your shirt, bear yourself upright, smiling and full of the sun in your bones.

I asked the driver to pass by the county jail, that place of early desperation. I had survived, and I wanted to throw it the finger in defiance.

When I came out of that place, an indigent, I found a room above a nightclub where blues bands wailed until four in the morning. The tenants in the boardinghouse upstairs were vagrants, pimps, whores and drug dealers. We shared the one bathroom and I would run into them all there: the dudes in their Superfly plumed hats and cashmere trench coats; the women peacocked with black eyeliner, fluffy boas and metallic-flaked spiked heels; the drunks passed out and snoring in their empty bottles.

One of the friends I made there was an ex-con who was obsessed with overhauling his car. All over his room, on the bed and from floor to ceiling, were strewn greasy parts from the engine, grills, bumpers, car seats, mirrors. Tools were scattered everywhere, and pieces of polished chrome and metal impeccably shining, and there was a pungent smell of machine grease, fluids, and acids. Out back in the alley, the hulking frame of the car, freshly primed, sat under a street lamp.

Each morning we had to go to a clearinghouse and wait to be called for work on the trucks that delivered food to the welfare centers. Days they didn't call us, we played pool;

then back to our rooms, where my friend would sit and tinker with his car parts, and I'd head for my steel-framed bed that shuddered and pinged when the guitarist and drummer downstairs rehearsed a rhythm. At night I'd walk the beach, or stand on the pier and watch the waves roll in as gulls pecked at the leftover food of picnickers. By the time I got back, the whole building would be shaking and rattling in an earthquake of blaring music.

Another con I hung with was Rudy, a Chicano boxer just out of the county jail. One night we were shooting pool at a billiard hall and these two Chicanas were playing at the next table. Some rowdy guys were at the bar drinking pitchers of beer and they started to hassle the women. Rudy punched one of them out and the other two jumped in. I jumped for Rudy. We left with the girls, who warned us not to go back there because the guys we beat up were some gang-bangers. As we drove away, we saw scores of seething bikers heading for the pool hall to avenge their friends. Rudy and I signed the cross.

I felt nervous. Other times a chauffeured ride had meant federal marshals or the cops taking me to prison. I felt like going to East L.A. and asking the driver to cruise a bit, let them hydraulics rear and kick down the streets. I rolled my window down so people could see me, and asked the driver to stop and pick up a six-pack. I used the car phone to make a long distance call home and tell them how I was uppin' it now. What I really wanted was to ride on to Mexico and never be heard from again.

The limo dropped me at the Beverly Hilton Hotel, where for the next few weeks I worked on my script with Taylor, the director and producer. It would be another two years before we started filming.

When I lived in East L.A., I saw a whole country of brown-faced people. Living among them had made me want to say things I always want to say when I'm on stage reading my poetry and giving lectures. I would have liked to say to those thousands of brown faces that L.A. is not about stars, not about Hollywood. That every creative life-form we know started as a seed in the heart of someone like them. It's not about what's out there, but what's in here, in the heart. Fight against the abuses, stand up and take your chairs and break them, get that rage out of you; then let the warrior in your hearts rest, let the wise one in the soul stand and speak and eloquently rail against the injustices until you are heard.

I wanted to talk about the police beating Chicanos with impunity on the streets of L.A., and about the safe academics who can't stand our guts. I wanted to say that in INS* camps *méjicanos* get bludgeoned by border patrols, that our civil rights are violated everywhere by foul racists. And mostly I wanted to say, nay shout, with a deep booming voice that cannot be ignored: Rise, Chicano Nation and take your rightful place, burn down those doors that are barred against you because of your color, your language. Step out on the streets, the millions of you, and sing your love, sing it so that windows burst and women and children and men hold hands again: let your immense and beautiful power be seen and heard.

It's all in the heart, the suffering, in all the tears we've shed over the meaningless deaths and drive-bys, in the funeral laments, in the sad *cantinas* and the prisons filled with men with broken hearts and limping spirits. I want to awaken the Chicano Nation to fly like a bird to the spring and drink from the sweet flowers of freedom scintillating with nectar. I want us to take back our right to live with honor and dignity. I wanted to say, if they don't give them to you, then *take* your rights. No one else can speak for you, no one else can give you justice, no one else can stop the violence, no one can ensure that your civil rights are respected: *you* must do it.

There's a potential power that lingers over the night streets

---

*Immigration and Naturalization Service

of L.A. like ocean mist blown in from a faraway island carrying ancient remembrances of who I am, who we are. And I know L.A. is mean and lonely, but what you believe in and can create there will give meaning to your life. You must believe in your trip, even though thousands of heavy trips that oppose it are happening around you every minute. Believe in what you do and who you are.

L.A. is an automobile culture, and I abhor the traffic snarls as much as the next man. But there is a certain high I get coming off the ramp at sixty, while around me, from horizon to horizon, guard rail to guard rail, six frenzied lanes of bumper-to-bumper cars are jockeying to get where they're going. Nowhere in the world is it so crazy, and yet I love to jump in, gas pedal floored, adrenaline pumping; and when I start to race-drive, threading in and out, I feel the giddiness of a kid in his go-cart flying down a steep hill. A drive down the L.A. freeways is a great communal therapy session. Everybody is babbling into phones, dreaming of Caribbean vacations, plotting divorces, lusting for their lovers, worrying about the house they can't make payments on: and the thousands of cars around them are just backdrops to these private scenes.

After a late script session, I was driving home through West Hollywood. It was Friday night and the light-loafers were out. I stopped at a red light and some gays were crossing the street. One of them stopped on the median. He had lush blond curls and red blusher on his cheeks and darkened lashes. He bent over to untie his shoelaces, then to slowly retie them: a fevered sexual display. Under the green and red lights, he was starring in his own movie. I drove on, past men on street corners babbling to small crowds, pouring verbal graces on their listeners, and quasi-prophets conjuring disaster on the heads of unbelievers.

The lights on Sunset burn like location lighting, creating cinema stars of the anonymous faces. Later their names are tenderly whispered from lipsticked lips in dark corner booths where dreams waterfall and lovers stroke each other's ego as they empty bottle after bottle of designer waters and fancy wines. Later still, slowly, they will strip to bare thighs and breasts and cocks, while their breath swelters thick with romance and tongues twine in long, sensuous stereo-orchestrated kisses--until dawn light flushes the blinds and the performance ends.

In L.A. you share in a million stories through the music pulsing from open doors and windows, and the movie marquees and placards of upcoming attractions. They're all out there—the young risktakers and the gamblers, the talent agents and stars. And the city has a bilingual heart: in L.A. you live in two worlds, in celluloid shadows and hard reality. L.A. is South Americans whirring weed cutters on mansion grounds; old hippies with small boy's features toddling naked in their gardens at dawn; crowds of workers on street corners hiring out to a different employer every day. It is a city of the homeless sleeping in alleys on discarded couches, and single people living in fifty-room palaces on million-dollar-a-month budgets. There you become a two-world person, inhaling the intoxicating perfume of luxury and extravagance, and turning away from the piercing sight of poverty. Los Angeles miraculously replenishes itself by drinking in dreams. It's where life runs on opposites, greed and generosity; it's where the fire of envy consumes the heart of an actor burning to step over his fallen friend's bad luck to take his turn in the cold reach for stardom.

Los Angeles is a whale's blowhole spouting the flickering blue imaginations that drench America's dreams; a flight into the darkness of the heart; a brief reprieve from the harsh light of necessity. It's a city that collects the big names the way a kid collects baseball cards. The wild chance, the gamble on suddenly becoming crazy rich or crazy poor, thrusts you into a primal dance of carnivorous hunger. It is the great candy shop for men and women who refuse to grow up; and it breaks up, chews and spits out families who try to live decent lives there. It's a place where the heart sports gold-studded black leather. L.A. is a funky twenties nightclub with a flashing neon sign, where a jazzy blues singer wails and the regulars are shipwrecked pirates, priests and poets, with more culture and savvy than money. L.A. is a night that ends with your heart charged to create again all your lost dreams, where you walk barefoot in the sands, the ocean at your side, singing the pain in your soul as only the ocean can.

And when you wake, L.A. is an erotic white '57 Chevy that you have to hot-wire, impeccable white upholstery trimmed with black, voluptuously marbled and phallic, trimwork chromed, that glimmers and cruises the Sunday parks, its muffler blowing newspapers across empty parking lots, and you are the news. And everyone wants the keys to that car, they want to drive it to the limits of frenzied fantasy; but something could go wrong, you could get caught, it's not your car, after all, even though they let you drive it past your friends to boost your ego. But L.A. is not yours, it belongs to the imagination.

Yet when you engage the gears, and feel the vibration of L.A. between your thighs and its heat in your loins, L.A. turns you on like nothing else can; and the incredible power of the engine and the glow and the speed and the feeling of freedom can make you believe that car is yours. So you take the curves too fast, imagining that what you touch will turn to gold, that everything you see is yours and the magnetic axis of the world is tilting toward you every prize you ever dreamed of.

But those who buy this delusion get infected with a deadly disease. You can see them on the talk shows pronouncing judgments, and labeling inequities with righteous pontifical fingers. Lost in their private myths, their every speech is a tribute to themselves, homage to their puny power, as they wallow in corpses of yesterday's gossip columns. For them L.A. is a condor's dream, a place where they eat the flesh of young dreamers, destroying their power to act. They are the condors who crack out of the shells of asphalt streets to sharpen their beaks on the young, with cold appetite feeding their false life on youth's hot vitality.

And after all is said and done, you look out the window and see the car parked where it was before, a napkin on the floor bearing the imprint of a lover's lipstick, keys in the ignition, enticing you still to turn the lock—and ride.

L.A. is a freshly lanced blister of ugly buildings, and ripe out-of-reach dreams luring you from the topmost tree-branches. Reaching beyond my grasp, learning to fly by falling, I suspend my hummingbird soul over the city to be filled with the city's poems. And my hands are red with its blood, my heart seared with urban madness, and brim with desolation.

The night is aromatic with citrus dew and the ocean opens waves for lost dreamers turned down by casting directors, for Mexicans yearning for home, for the penniless young who have come to this last coast to escape from their tragic secrets back home. I twine my python imagination around the waist of an avocado tree, flickering my tongue of light faintly on the skin of an L.A. moon. And as I bite into her tropical heart, whose pain is a soft glow language cannot fathom nor the spirit imagine, Bite me, L.A. whispers, Bite me.

V
Jazz Riffs

Making Do—
Chicano Style

It seemed that Victor had gone from lower-class *vato* to high-class aristocrat when he phoned to inform me that he had bought a boat.

"A boat?" I visualized a rusty canoe picked up at a yard sale. In arid New Mexico, boats are more status symbols than of practical use.

"Yep," he said, "a big boat with a drooling Chrysler engine, thirsty for water . . ."

Often Victor and I carry on together like a couple of comedians. Nothing is safe from our mockery. It's good therapy in a world where ninety-five percent of Chicanos live way below the poverty line.

So we kidded about the boat, how it was just the beginning of big things ahead—island-hopping around the world in private jets, custom-made suits, beautiful women, fine wines. . . . It was all there for the taking for the boat owners of the world, or, in my case, the *primos* of boat owners. Onassis Baca—has a nice ring.

Victor said his boat had a downstairs and an upstairs, and gloated at length about the powerful engine. I was impressed. We made plans to take it out to Blue Water Lake the following weekend and baptize it with its first run in fifteen years. You could say that piece of information might have made me think twice. But then, you weren't on the other end of Victor's euphoria.

It seems that the boat had been dry-docked in somebody's yard, where it did duty as a shelter for barrio dogs and birds' nests. Now it was a big conversation piece for *vatos* stopping by to see Victor. Ownership of a boat in the barrio in New Mexico says either that you work for the government and get a good two-week check, or that you screwed someone out of some money and can't be trusted. But Victor has a way of dancing to his own tunes, and if anyone could pull off a sweet deal like this it was Victor.

I hadn't seen Victor in fifteen years when I returned one day to Albuquerque, leathered out and riding my Harley Davidson. My hair was long, my pockets stuffed with drugs, my life a heap of chimney ash in the black dustpan of the day. There was some kind of protest rally happening downtown by the convention center and the police had put up a roadblock. So I idled my scooter, cursing the crowds who were slowing me down in getting home to smoke my white dragon heroin and blow the coke stash in my pocket.

And there before me, as I snarled at the marchers, was my *primo* Victor. He was much taller and older than the other protestors, and togged out in baggy green khakis and plaid shirt, a heavy sheepskin sweater and sneakers. I yelled out, "Yeah, you! Victor! What the fuck are you doing, *vato*?" Ever since that day we've shared a lot of stomach-aching happy laughter and embraces and crazy journeys into the mountains—a whole lot of hell-raising.

So, knowing Victor, I wasn't really surprised by the boat. I knew it would bring us some exciting times. He'd be taking the week to get it in shape, doing odds and ends to make it fit for the trial run. Since he'd gotten a good deal on it, he was able to spend a little money to trim it out.

Saturday came. My sons, who were coming with us, were racing around the house with excitement. I had told them that not just anyone owns a boat, that owning a boat was proof we had made it: even if it wasn't exactly ours, at least we had a boat-owning friend. The warm glow of success was upon me. My sons thought I was crazy, seeing as how they really are smarter than I am, but they indulged their papa who was driving them to Victor's on fumes and with about a dollar and twenty cents to his name.

I was picturing myself on future trips, basking on deck in my flash shades and enjoying a view of my wife getting tan in her bikini, the drink in my hand tilted in such a manner as to affect ultimate sophistication. Truth is, the closest I've come to tilting my wrist is holding my wooden fishing rod steady to light a cigarette in such a way as not to disturb the fishline and scare away the fish. But that was in the preboat era. I was sure that now, fishing off a boat, I would catch the biggest trout ever. I had always regarded with envy the people who steered their boats out to the prime fishing spots while, on the shore, I was getting my line tangled in the rubbish left behind by yahooing weekenders. This boat would put me right on top in the world of anglers.

At Blue Water, I was to be responsible for the kids while Victor took the wheel. We went aboard carrying a cooler filled with picnic foods and soft drinks, and soon we were all glistening with suntan lotion. Now we were truly living the American dream. All around us were water-borne suburbanites, their trailers and Winnebagos parked around the camping grounds. When anyone came within earshot of us, I yelled out an affable howdy.

We were all set to go. Victor pushed the button confidently to crank the motor—but all that he got were some sluggish snorts and burps of black smoke. Captaining the controls, he ordered me to yank the rope around the pulley wheel. It could jump, he warned, and he gripped the wheel and leverage, his feet squarely planted on the deck. After some manly rips, the motor started—then wheezed and went dead.

But Victor was prepared. He had brought along a portable battery and cables in case of just such contingencies. I was totally impressed by his foresight. At his direction, I put the cables on the good battery and ran them to the motor to jump-start the thing. Trying to maintain my balance as the boat rocked and bobbed, I cranked the pulley wheel, snagging up the battery cables a few times in the process. Finally, I managed to connect the pliers to the poles, even though one of the pliers kept slipping.

As I stood there ankle-deep in water, Victor imparted the news that the boat had only one speed, full blast. Sure enough, when the engine finally fired and he put it into gear, the nose reared up and I found myself up to the elbows in water. When the boat suddenly lurched, I was nearly thrown overboard, and got so disoriented I had trouble keeping my balance. For a minute the world seemed to be all churning water, as I struggled to find the battery poles and clamp on my pliers so the boat wouldn't die again. I was going to keep this boat going no matter what. Through all of this I maintained my faith that Victor knew what he was doing. That's friendship.

I surfaced from the water with all the bravado of Captain Ahab hunting the monster whale and yelled at Victor to slow down—we were really moving now. Ignoring my plea, Victor yelled back an order to hold the cables to the battery: we were going to get out and do some fishing! Well, he was the captain. . . .

By this time I was drenched by the big waves that kept slapping on board. I began, a little late, to realize that Victor was not so much dominating the boat as the boat, reeling wildly back and forth, was dominating Victor, who had all he could do just to hold on to the wheel. Through the sheets of spray blurring my vision, I saw three smiling children's faces—Victor's son was with us—staring at me from the cabin.

At some point in this mythic struggle, it occurred to me that I stood a good chance of getting electrocuted if I kept my hold on the cables. I really didn't want to be the one reeled out of the water on a hook instead of a fish. So I started to shout to Victor my intention to let go. But when

I looked at him and saw how much fun he was having, grinning and fighting the controls, I didn't have the heart to mutiny.

It was fun for me too, landlubber that I am, to be living out one of those great sea stories, a seaman fighting for his life. In no time and very few miles, I felt I understood the perils and hardships endured by those intrepid sailors who had voyaged from Europe to America. If my courage failed me now, the tale of it would make me the scorn of every seaman's tavern from Blue Water Lake to Mexico City. But, if I held firm, my tale of heroism would rival that of Odysseus. Back in Burque, I would regale the *vatos* in epic style.

By now I could barely see through the sheets of spray sweeping over me. The tremendous force of the engine was plowing up great rocking waves of white water that seemed to be boiling over the whole surface of the lake. We were in a no-wake area, and off to the shore scores of fishermen were throwing us the finger and waving us away. Victor was manfully jerking the wheel back and forth, still trying to locate its center of balance. He wasn't making a very good job of it. As for me, I was doing all I could not to fly overboard. The boat was slapping the water hard, with violent thud, thud, thuds, charging straight ahead like a bull with a red flag before it. The kids were holding on for dear life in the cabin, fearless and thrilled with the roller coaster ride.

Suddenly I saw two lake patrols pulling out behind us, the red bulbs mounted on their boats revolving. I couldn't hear the sirens, but as they got closer I saw the officers motioning me to pull to the side. Anybody in his right mind could have noticed that I was trying everything in my power just to *see*—yet the officers' hostile gestures became more pronounced, as if I could perform a miracle. I translated their enraged gestures: Off to the side! Stop immediately! I wanted to dive into the water and disappear. Couldn't they see that I wanted the boat to stop even more than they did?

By this time I had let go of the cables and was clinging to the hull rail for dear life. The motor had seized on its highest speed and there it stuck. We were flying, barely skimming the surface of the water. Some of the time the boat was on its side, like a car making a turn on two wheels; other times the prow was straight up, with me underwater, then slapping down so hard that my senses reeled. Now a desperate Victor was tearing out wires and trying to pull off the steering wheel—*anything* to stop the boat. After what seemed like eons, I heard the motor gag, cough—and die. The patrol boats pulled closer and Victor and I exchanged looks: trouble ahead. The kids were choking on their laughter after a ride as thrilling as any Magic Mountain coaster.

We were towed to shore.

Victor was ticketed for destruction of government property. He had ripped down several bob-ropes and signs. It came out that he had no registration, no boat license, no safety permit, no life jackets; they threw the book at him. The tickets amounted to more than twice what the boat was worth.

On the ride back to Albuquerque, Victor and I asked each other how it all could have happened. I mean, the whole thing about having the boat, and not really being able to afford a boat, and getting into debt over one boat ride, was weird. It's kinda sad, this life of ours, kinda sad, we agreed.

Still, you'd have to call it a day to remember. . . .

Dog Blues

When I left New Mexico to spend time working on a film script in Los Angeles, my dog Baby already was headed for trouble. A few times in the past couple of years, he had squirmed through the holes in my neighbor's fence and chased her peaceful flock of sheep all over the fields. I would be in the house playing with the kids, or writing in my office, and I would hear chickens squawking and geese honking and dogs barking next door. It seemed to me that Baby was doing no harm, but my neighbor kept warning me that one day he was going to bite one of the sheep or kill a chicken. He had killed some chickens before, but when she asked if I had seen any of her Rhode Island hens, I never told my neighbor about the dead birds I had found in my yard. She was missing a couple.

Baby is a curious dog. I like big, barrelling-down-on-you dogs, with voracious appetites for robust play and gusty lunging. That's not Baby.

He is a mongrel mutt with a Buddha-like air of tranquility. He curls up in a corner of the house all day and never budges, and I tend to forget he's around. In fact, I don't care too much about him. To me he's something like a kid I would rather have in the Marines than have around, lying in his corner and eyeing me with that pitiful "please be kind to me" look.

One day a while back, my son came to tell me there

was a shaggy dog cowering in the weeds by the roadside near our house. I didn't know which looked worse, the scrawny weeds or this shaggy sack of shivering bones. If ever there was a being totally unlovable, there it was. I tried to convince my son that we didn't need another dog, we already had two dogs, two horses, one cat, rabbits and birds. But he felt sorry for it, so I told him that if he could lure the dog into our yard he could keep it. I figured it had been beaten mercilessly since birth and there was little chance my son could coax such a people-shy dog to approach us.

But, several days later, there was the dog, a huge ragged hair-ball spit out by a diseased lizard on its dying breath. He was lapping up the milk and food Antonio had put out for him and wagging his tail with every mouthful. But, when I came near, he sprinted off and rolled into a ball under a bench, in the dark.

Somehow, he stayed. He became part of the yard, half invisible, hanging at the margins and shyly testing the hospitality of his new friends. He was no problem, except for the occasional poaching into neighbors' yards sniffing for adventure.

Over the years, as I got to know him, he grew on me. I accepted his cowering, his shivering, meek attitude, his crawling up to me on his knees. He was a coward and that was okay. To this day he has never bounded up to me freely. He drags his ass and turns it sideways and pulls himself toward me with his two front paws. Then, when I say something nice to him, he immediately turns belly up and surrenders— every time. So I have never been able to pet his back, it's always his belly. I could let this get to me, but it's him, what the hell, he is who he is.

Recently, however, he has taken on more importance in the family. Here is this creature called Baby, a dog we never wanted but adopted anyway and grew to love—I with some questioning of my sanity, for there is nothing lovable about him. He is a coward, pure and simple, with no intention of making himself useful; he doesn't even bark. He is incapable of scaring any intruder, even a mouse.

True, he loves to follow my sons when they go bike riding; and he never commits any horrible transgressions, like tearing up the rose garden, or shitting in the house. But now he is a felon with a rap sheet. (The innocent always go first.)

Not long ago my wife called to tell me Baby had bitten a sheep and had been hauled away to the dog pound. Fine. We could bail him out, give him a good whack, and that would be that. But then the problem began to compound, as problems always do when you least expect it. The vet bill was two hundred dollars. Now, you can buy a sheep in New Mexico for thirty dollars, but our neighbor wouldn't sell us the sheep. Then the wound got maggots in it and became infected. Another two-hundred-dollar bill from the vet.

There I was, wildly pacing my room in L.A., asking myself why I ever took the dog in, while my sons were solely preoccupied with breaking Baby Face out of jail. And so often did they remind me that he would soon be put to death unless we saved him, that I started to call my older boy "Antonio Hacksaw Baca." Antonio and Gabriel now had only one mission in life: to spring Baby Face.

But first we—meaning me—had to pay his bail. Which I did. The day before his execution date, he was free. Another seventy-five dollars. The pound administrators informed me I now had to have him checked out by a vet. Seventy dollars more.

My wife, having decided that we couldn't keep Baby at home because he would go after the sheep again, tried to find someone who would take him, but to no avail. So there was nothing else to do but buy a carrying cage for him and fly him out to me in L.A. But first to the beauty salon to shampoo him, fluff him up for Hollywood, prune his claws (did he even have claws?), and then—my skin crawled with disbelief—buy him a ticket on USAir which cost more than I pay myself to fly alley-scuffle business class on Southwest.

The cage cost me one hundred dollars; the beauty salon another fifty; and the airline ticket another hundred. And now, months later as I write this, I look down at my feet and there is Baby Face, lying on his side and blissfully sleeping in the West Coast sunshine.

Nothing about him has changed. He still comes to me dragging his ass as if his back legs don't know how to stand, and every time he approaches me it's ass-first, in the same old cowardly way. Although he is all but invisible still, wanting nothing, becoming nothing, in a state of dog bliss, everywhere I look are tiny balls of white fur that defy the vacuum cleaner. People come to visit, and I read in their eyes the judgment that I am too lazy to clean the carpet and that I enjoy living in squalor. I don't bother to tell them that for every one of the hundreds of tiny hair-balls I try to pick up three more appear. I wanted to keep him outside, but my kids tell me that would be cruel.

So people come to see me and they see my dog and gasp with pleasure, cooing over this perfect little angel whose flesh you could not find if you took a lawn mower to him. And somewhere beneath those layers and layers of matted and knotted hair is a dog whose eyes I have never seen, that stare out from thick vines of tangled hair; eyes that must be smiling the smile of benevolence that con artists keep for their marks after they've brought off a scam.

Give the dog a bone; he's earned it.

Journeys: Gleanings from a Poet's Journals

The road was very wide once and I was young-hearted.
Plenty of room for people to pass. No ruts or boulders to
roughen the passage. I ran and sped, carefree.

And then drugs entered my life and the road narrowed.
From an open passageway, leading to any dream I chose, it
became a one-car road, rutted, ominous, shrouded in shadows.
Suddenly I no longer knew the road. There was less and less
room to maneuver, to move out of the way of oncoming traffic
blinding me with headlights. Every waking day became a risk,
a game of chance, a desperate attempt to find a high that
was better than my own breathing, my own pounding heart.
This is a story of that road and of how, at the end of it,
there was the signpost: DEAD END.

It begins in 1978. I am sitting in a house in Vancouver,
Canada. I have just been released from prison. No parole,
no probation, no half-way house. From a maddening, insulated,
brutal environment, I have exited, free, with a bus ticket, and
every road open.

For months I have been writing to a woman, and through
our letters we have agreed I will come and live with her. It's
an old re-run—convict meets woman, released from prison
he goes to her, the movie ends.

I am in her house, a two-story country mini-palace, with
sprawling grounds, surrounded with lush woods, dotted with
silvery lakes. I am stunned, dazed by my long confinement.
Days blur into months as I walk the grounds like a prince,

take deer paths in the woods. The lakes are circles of dreamy silver moons nestled in humid woods.

I dare not reflect on my past. I dare not acknowledge what my life means. To feel the hurt and pain would scorch me. Better to be numb, blot out the garden of horrors seeded, blossomed and digested in prison, blind myself to the man I became there. Be numb, forget. Let the garden wilt and die of neglect. I am in a state of emotional drought; my feelings baked clay in her hands, in which I scratch and claw for sustenance. I have done it too, until my fingers bled. And then at some unmarked hour, on a pale blue afternoon, I became a wasteland where hours collected like robed travelers in the desert and died. Sand covered their skeletons, covered the roads going in and coming out; and my breath became as blowing dust, effacing all hope of return to the green lush place of my innocence.

There was a pool of poison in me, a rabid growl in the marrow. A fatal sense of defeat at being a human assaulted me. I could not touch, smell, see, hear, or taste, except through the gloved covering of anger that scaled my senses, well-fashioned in defense against people and the intruding world that had violated me, humiliated me, until my soul was a ravaged battlefield.

Ask me how a man is healed and I will tell you it depends on the damage he has endured. Imagine a snowfall in which each flake is a razor blade, nicking your skin, your face and arms, until speckles of blood bead every inch of your flesh with hardly-visible incisions. Those flakes are the minutes I endured, each minute flying at me silvery-thin unseen, a night fall of millions of flakes, every inch of me smarting from a million wounds. How a night of soft snowfall could turn away from me its innocent face as though I was diseased, and turn to me instead the snarling nightmare underside of beauty and innocence . . . The only recourse then is to cut off all feeling, to become numb—and pay the terrible consequence of that later.

1/12/89
ALBUQUERQUE

CHANGE: NOW & BEFORE

After meeting with two funding sources yesterday, I was so happy with the success that I lost my center. I wanted to make calls and party. Get high after every success? I was dispossessing my spirit. I needed to rub my spirit in dirt, put my voice back in my body, and tell the spirits I was home again. I stopped alongside the road, burned cedar, and prayed to the four directions. . . .

Miracle happened. . . .

1/13/89
BIG SUR

FOR JIM AND MEGHAN

> I can't imagine a life without crying, she said,
> and quoted, "Eyes that have not cried
>   are like a soul that has not seen a
>   rainbow."

I climb up the paved road from their house,
over a mound, top the mountain,
then heel down a sharp steep curving road.
Cross the road.
I couldn't find a path down—
barred by thorned brush, scented peppermint.
Turn back
and sit now on the boulder, looking out over the vast blue

sea.

I wonder if the ocean feels pain,
in its contstant thrashing and whispering roar-capped
slings—
    so wide and broad blue
    foiling waves upon
    a thorny rock crop.

    The sun is warm here.
    Grit sprays over my face.
Does it feel pain of not seeing or knowing the desert?

            It does.
            Everything is change.
It has been the desert in after-ages,
and I will see my tears
    beat against the black rock someday
    the door of stone
    that lies on my heart
    whose red roots slowly crack through
    the crevices.

"A few times in my life I have felt a powerful
surge in me rise, from stomach to chest, and
I breathed it back down," I said.

        Looking at the ocean now,
        I wonder when I weep,
        will I sit on the
                        rocky precipice of my old life,
        wondering in awe at the marvel
        of what tears have cleared away
        for me to see?
        Will tears bring in to me
        old shipwrecked debris of journeys
        I have taken and never finished,
        of dreams I went after
        but never found,

                will salty tears,
                tears,
                        do this?
Will there be two continents
roughly divided if I cry,
one where I have been,
trekked the deep tread of pain
endlessly,

the other offering where I have not been,
open water to follow
where I will?

                On an endless course
                of exploring
                my being, my poor being?

I pity a man like myself,
who has depended so much on not crying
to survive in this life—
                and yet,
                each memory is an oar
                that only needs me
                to push off from shore
                steering myself back down
                the shady river
                my life is. Only me.
                Coming back to where I started—
                that clearing full of dead trees
                where I left my last cry
                like a cairn of burnt stones
                that warmed me when the night was
                long, and I lost myself
                and didn't know how to find my way
                out.

Startle myself with the oceans
that have formed here.

My blood beats against the black door
          of *no cry*,
and every time I needed a word to
describe the pain,
          I cried *no cry*
no cry to describe the fear,
no cry to pain,
until the words
          no cry
          built themselves up
          to a steep cliff,
          no way down
          but to fall
                    fall
                              fall
          back down

          to cry.

1/14/89
SANGRE DE CRISTO MOUNTAINS

A THOUGHT

I learned the value of life by being in circumstances that systematically abuse it, and with people who indulged their dead and degraded souls by denigrating others.

I too was not immune from this. Places in me shut down, closed. Ideas and feelings rusted, corrugated coagulations that stopped the spirit from flowing out and hardened the senses.

But what has saved me, I think, is the slender shoot of

spiritual light that has often pierced the darkness, and I have moved toward it to feel light-warmth in the darkness. This small opening of light has saved me, made me imagine another possibility of being.

Because of this small opening, I have opened myself small too, small hairline cracks of hope and faith describe the surface of my heart's terrain. And this has led me to trust people when I otherwise wouldn't have had the courage. Has given me strength to see, touch, feel and accept genuine human love when I have encountered it.

No value was ever given me, of such beauty, until I experienced its ugly side. Among mad men, I have always found one sane one and bared my soul to him. Like a boy finding his best friend dead and leaving him in a field, I kept on walking over plains and hills until I found another one who had left his dead friend, and, on meeting, we embraced, disbelieving, full of awe at human life, blossoming together in the soil of death to further life.

I know what I know because of what I've seen of hard times—and those soft, rare moments of good times—those miraculous chance meetings of soulmates, in the most inconceivable circumstances, that can be understood only as operations of life's driving force of love, to create out of darkness hope. Nurture me, Great Grandfather, in my darkness, help me upward from roots into blossom.

I make strong roots now. I no longer sink them into air. Roots must be germinated in darkness, in quiet, in depths of contemplation.

1/16/89
STANFORD

A NOTE ON FRIENDS

I have friends all over the earth. All colors, speaking all languages, men and women and children.

Imagine I am very soft ground. When I start out, soft mulch, worked in the abdomen, a birthing ground, dirt flesh, soft under foot, catching stray seeds, wind-blown seeds. And my attachment to mountain paths is strong: bark chips, black wet dirt, ferns, wild lush vegetation—these are part of me.

It is a wide world. And one chooses the paths one will take. Somehow, I found it in myself to stray from soft ground. Here and there I saw broken glass fragments. I followed the broken glass path until more and more littered the path. The glittering sheen of glass became more important to me than soil.

The nice soft ground path was gone.
Why did I choose broken glass friends,
each footstep drawing pain and blood,
incurring wounds? Why?

I will not talk about
atmosphere. How leafy bird-voiced trees
became barren gray dead stark
threatening hulks of menace—
not that.

But speak on good friends—
how it takes time to find them,
how each step at a time
leads me back to me,
to the softness underfoot that is me,
cloaked in dew.
I evaporate into leaves, branches, animals
breathe me,
earth exhales and inhales me,
molding herself of me
not broken glass and blood.

It is not all or nothing. Remember that.

Ok to sleep late, have nothing to do,
look out window, listen, feel, think,
if you're doing something—ok.
>Wake up late.
>You are doing nothing.
>Something works on me,
>comes in me,
>forms from without—
>ok
to be part plant, tree, leaf,
a stone,
letting air, sun, woods, silence
root in you
and blossom a feeling of being.
A few days later, I run
miles and feel startled from the languor of non-being,
my vigorous strides,
my breath easy,
my strength and endurance enormous,
after doing nothing-work.

Those hours of sadness
of prolonged intimacy with oneself
are good. Thirsting, I wait,
feel a need to drink.
It takes time to know good friends.
To earn them, to know them, to appreciate them.
Time. You. Silence.
Go easy. Wait.
You will find you are not running
from yourself, but in harmony with your shadow self,
that person and those many people on
the other side of the words,
who you draw out from their shadow world, past
the screen of paper. Through the mirror of paper,
the white smoking mirror,

they arrive worded strong, glad, with plenty of energy.
A seed that has germinated in moist black silence—
spread legs out in long strides,
feel the soft ground underfoot,
watch out for broken glass.
The choice is yours. Mine. Ours.

Go slow.
Pace yourself.
Do not think of distance.
Friends are forever.
Freedom.

1/19/89
NEW YORK

THE POEM'S PROCESS

On writing a poem.

I have a friend. Both his legs were broken. I went to the hospital three times a week to help him through his rehabilitative workouts. We cried, laughed, cursed, clenched our fists, grunted and grieved. But, one day, he struggled through the horizontal bars, the same hands that caressed his children's lips, his lover's breasts, now gripped the wooden bars, and step by step, day by day, expressed the creative faith in life, a little more each day. When I saw his face contorted with painful effort, I wept. Pleasure in his triumph at moving a toe made me yelp. I watched him struggle, lifting up his braced right foot slowly, easing it down, then the left foot— up—down. He had been a quiet man, a welder, and one day the strap on a tractor-trailer snapped, and thousands upon thousands of iron pipes crushed his legs. And now I was witnessing how sheer will and love of life carried more force than all that iron weight, as this beautiful angel of a man challenged the odds to win.

Working on a poem is like this, I thought, as I left the hospital one day. One walks through it painfully, never feeling the full limbered ease of mastery over it, but between one word and the next one inches forward, full of pleasure and fiery pain. We pull and strain forth, until we walk through the poem and call ourselves back from its green depths the way we once were.

The joy of finishing a poem is like a breaking of braces, being suddenly freed and skipping, dashing along an open expanse of field, whirling, the arteries become Scottish bagpipes as one spins in the open clearing of the finished poem.

Moving from lip-biting pain to exhilarating pauses of pleasure, learning to respect the basics of grammar, of structure, to go step by savoring step, walking into the poem, writing to become a better man, and for no other reward.

1/19/89
YALE

POETIC ESTHETICS

Know that all of us have a metaphor, an image map, a myth stamped in our soul that describes our life pattern. I feel mine, under the fog of my passions, the blue emotions, rugged peaks of reason in the pristine clear spring beneath my soul: this is my metaphor. My poems are the palpitating nerve-endings of that journey to touch my life-metaphor, and the closer I get to my myth, this cosmic-precast of my life's destiny, the more my life resonates with truth and creativity, with a ripe sense of fulfilling my destiny.

I feel that way now, flying over the Sierras, snowy pine-treed furred Sierras; I feel I am mapping my way back to my lost self, penetrating the I-cave from which my poetry issues, this myth-metaphor of me in this life, blending into the moving boundaries of all other life, co-existing with mountains, snow, desert, feeling their being more deeply the closer I come to mine.

◆

PHILOSOPHY

My life is like preparing a meal
when I will be most hungry—
on my death bed,
I want the nourishment that a soul hungers for
when looking back, knowing
there is a long way to go.

2/2/89
SAN FRANCISCO

There is a strong connection between nature's roots, leaves, seasons, and the patterns of my own growth. The dark abysm of growth. The terrible dark gleam in Pound's eyes as he existed at St. Elizabeth's asylum. That haunted look, which I have studied for hours now, sitting in my room, of the condemned, that falls upon all poets who do not strive for truth and tell it in their work. In Pound's eyes I see the dark abysm and gloom of death-in-life. We are stems of strange songs, stems of foliage, spark-petals and star-dancers in the darkness of our forward motion.

Pound frowned—a fragmented man. A man whose tendril roots blew in the ward, through the concrete walls, above the sea, folding inward to root in the cosmic debris, collapsing,

exploding its density
bulking convulsions

to form into star-poems
lustrous ancient gold dazzle.
In the rat-infested barrio
song-shine
in my heart
poems human formed.

◆

Print—
each letter is a star
in this darkness
I grope in.
I travel this journey
with faith, staking all I am
in search for meaning
in the darkness
between words,
between letters.

I become part of others
by sharing the space between letters,
choose the endless seeing
part of them,
it is all
        blending
hybrid
        blossoms.

Breathing
holding hands
in a song
of living
words that describe me
describe the universe.
Language of the flower

of stone
is my God
tongue.

The dark shadow
on the field
appears
     I must travel now
     into pre-breath
     to form myself, my voice, into a dance of butterflies
     in wind
     fluttering down a mesa.

What are poems?

     Peyote buttons
     black rocks in a sweat lodge
     turned red
     my soul steams off
     floating at dawn

     I'll become today.

(Each poem is a black rock
 we heat
 with our energy
 'til it turns red
 and cold water of our dreams
 steam off its burning surface.)

♦

POETIC PROCESS IS A RITUAL

Communion of silence
     making silence a black swan

and I glistening blue
                    forest water
    it floats upon.

◆

[A photograph in the dark]
"referring to tears . . ."
        Some people cry
        others don't.
                They make oceans
                to journey over,
                to see new shorelines.

◆

Chicano poetry was not accepted for a long time. My culture
was ignored or denied access to publishing, while others were
respected and given preference.

        While the rest of the world took photographs
        in the day
        I was taking photographs in the dark,
        seeing the hidden,
        capturing the soul in its darkness, its
        dream state,
        its ease
                like the infant's sleeping face
                framed in dark and moonlight
        not the smiling
                bland faces of broad daylight. . . .

CRAFT AND IMAGE—PURSUING A DEFINITION

On the work I am doing with images. What's happening in *Martin [& Meditations on the South Valley]*.

The eye looks forward, and at the eye's edge a shadow passes, at the corner—while the eye looks on the page, the image slides past, there is peripheral cognition on another level, awareness of shadow, the image works in darkness, not in light.

Think of levels in the brain—the recognition panels set up like this: IIII. The first panel is reason, the second panel symbol, etc. Way at the back, the image triggers the last panel, the panel that registers dreams, contains archetypal patterns, the panel that mostly works on dreams.

The eye flutters wildly as if sleeping, observing a dream. The nerves react to the dream image, you're reading the poem but the images work peripherally, sliding past the corner of the eye, activating the back panel of the brain. The eye flutters, goes back and forth as if seeing a dream (the poem), seeing image in a dream series, a dream texture, and triggering deep shadowy responses in the nerves.

The images are colorful and trigger a part of the mind that is almost all dream or birth-marks, birth-giving.

> Suddenly, the image opens its interior rain-blood,
> its dream-rain, its star-shower
> of animal energy
> and the inner eye flies within the image,
> cognition or seed germination.
>
> The inner eye picks it up, views the dream image,
> the body landscape of long ago,
> like a bulbflash in nighttime photography

where borders extend
to the sleeping face
caught in a flash of the spirit, groping in the darkness,
risking, vulnerable, as it steps into unknown, and
there flashes again an image, developing, catching
our nightmare and dreams,
our fears, our sublime tenderness and sleep
in this life.

3/1/89
BERKELEY

DISCUSSION WITH AZEE FROM SOUTH AFRICA AT BREAKFAST

When a man is stripped of everything—emotional, cultural, mental, and material, stripped of everything that defines and celebrates our humanity—and nothing is left to him but utter darkness—then the primal scream comes, and it permeates language: language, the only vehicle that can contain and convey birth.

The spirit flashes, revealing aspects of the
world in a sublime purpose
to his own life.
If a person does not risk or reach
he dies emotionally, mentally, and sometimes physically.

Barrio is an uncut diamond
encrusted with lots of outgrowths.
The poet's job is to find the cleavages
in this rough gem,
to hold it up to the sun
in all its brilliant beauty.

3/16/89
BOULDER

Question: When do you write poems?
Answer: If an infant cries in the dark, you pick it up.

3/27/89
SAN ANTONIO

IMAGES

1) They come out of strength; out of crushing humility at seeing oneself shattered, foolish, and wasted. Insight, as opposed to out-sight. Inscape as opposed to outscape. What is in there?

2) You must understand that there exist no pat formulas for mapping out one's journey. The myth in all of us is spectacular—its content is active metamorphosis. We cannot stand outside ourselves and analyze our growth—we are part of its organic development—we are becoming the image. It is a nameless lord that has come from the nameless land in which we search for our names, our faces: we are the land becoming.

3) Pain is the sunshine we grow by
joy of revelation our continuing sustenance
that nourishes our vision to go another step.

◆

IN THE VOID—KNOWLEDGE OF SELF

a) Relevant associations—intuitive links. (It's the *click* that thrust us forth—.) Think backwards. Break the pattern.

b) Naivety is a must. (As opposed to what we're told.)

c) Validate flashes of intuition and live by them.

d) You must reside on the *dreamside*—myths come from dream zone.

e) Reflection is everything. Peaceful time.

f) Who you are now has preceded the image of your true self—what you saw before, what you dreamed.

g) Graft yourself, your sensibilities to the tissue of image—body instincts.

h) Images are picture-messages that trigger radical changes of consciousness, they are events your life is ceremony of, celebrating you in germination.

i) Things happen without warning—differently than what you imagined.

j) What do you want to do? You have to risk.

k) Image and song healing predates all medicine.

l) What we can imagine ourselves we can become.

m) Perceive internal sounds, smells, tastes—images.

n) Engrave the darkness with our own impression.

o) Orient the imagery to what you need.

p) You are out there alone, a contact point the universe touches and recharges itself on. Recharge back.

q) Commitment and perseverance.

r) Interpretations? Curse changed to blessing.

s) Place, mood, feeling . . . random associations. Remember everything is an invention, a relatedness to you, your life, your weakness, compassion, strengths.

t) Encourage adventure by trust and dialogue.

u) Something is profoundly incomplete without your determination.

v) Self-remembering—your myth!

3/30/89
ALBUQUERQUE

NOTES FOR NOVEL
3 Items:

a) Telephones with four digits only, when you could still stick your head out the window and see your party-line neighbor.

b) Many once bought TVs. But they lived in such remote places no TV transmissions ever reached them, only white static snow. So they imagined pictures in the white snow. Look at it long enough, the mind projected forms and animals on the static. *That* was our show.

c) School days. How most of the activity centered on the water fountain. Water fountains, where lines formed, became the great town-meeting places for children.

3/31/89
ALBUQUERQUE

What more can I say. I don't think I have really said anything of importance. Everything is a sincere guess, a look at my life through the eyes of a child, a lizard, a flower.

4/1/89
SANTA FE PRISON

Met with the archbishop and we discussed metaphors. We need to revive the dormant power of our indigenous symbols. Every meeting of two people is a dance. Two languages of two peoples blended becomes a gift-giving. We need a renaissance of cultural folk practices.

4/2/89
LOS ANGELES

THOUGHT: Quest for Identity. Faith is sage ash burnt in a bronze cup crafted by an unknown field laborer. Smell the spicy scent of darkness fermenting, unknown fertility. Faith is a nail hammered in, but bent and hammered haphazardly.

4/3/89
NEW HAVEN

PREAMBLE TO READING AT YALE

I am but a speck in the sun-haze lighting the land. All these awards and degrees are driving you from your life. What if someone drove you away from your home? You have abandoned yourself.

Name ourselves tree, grass, sun.
Start over again from that point.

4/4/89
CHICAGO

AFTER READING AT BIG LOUIE'S BACKYARD

A young student asked me about my statement, something about fragility and strength, weren't they contradictory? Again I found the mind in the university is tuned to exclude, not integrate—things must be destroyed at the expense of singularity.

Fragility and strength find residence in harmony— anything harmonious has fragility and strength. A branch sways at the slightest breeze, but try to uproot a tree barehanded.

I can embrace my friend after working hard in the field all day, using strength to break dirt and arms to embrace.

We have been lied to too long and taught to live in such meager mental cubicles.

I embrace the widest and deepest possible experience, calling on each aspect of my experience as needed. The true center of such versatility lies in my faith and willingness to love and be loved.

◆

Be at the mercy of no one—be open.

◆

I have always been fascinated by clues.

◆

IDENTITY

I must describe how so much is welded in a moving mass toward progeny—who are we? What are those images that describe our soul's journey, and what effusive fragrance of faith is released that invigorates our life? I know it is spirit, but you must tread on holy space to find them. Those images are always near me, like the dark wispy shadows of a bird's wings above me that I catch only peripherally. I watch the bodiless shadow-wings of image flit across the grass. I am the body of dark-winged image-birds that fly out of the past to me.

4/10/89

CHILILI

THANK YOU SUN

I have been on a steady pedal to the metal drive for months. In and out of the house, meeting new people everywhere. I am staying with an old poet now for a few days. J has sad merry eyes, the kind that have seen black cedar drenched in dew in NM—open prairie dazzled with early frost. Butting about as a boy with big brogans on hard wood floors. He is rather reserved in attitude, laid back, *un vato con chingo de visión,* * who would rather not parade in front of the dart-throwing critics at Hispanic fairs.

There is a calm about him, his gestures are those of natural awakening . . . a seasoned man in the prime of ripeness. He's seen it all—the marches, the fights—and yet, at bottom, in his soul, he is a man on a lonely journey, a journey that finds him returning to simple things. He wears a vest, t-shirt, khaki bags, a stingy-brim, sunglasses, and black shoes. True in my eyes; in my soul he is a respected, reserved brother.

Many have tried to tear him down. Those Hispanics who claim Columbus as their father have tried to quell his spirit. Magazine editors, poets and writers who promote small-minded sell-out versions of Chicano culture.

◆

THOUGHT: Blind impetus of animal-heart energy—lunge into poetry!

◆

THOUGHT: Being a Chicano smells burnt. It is living from ashes to flame in life, not green tree-lined streets, but shadows

---

*A man with a lot of vision.

and flame, dancers around the fire, warring young, meditative old ones, healing with their words and love. The old ones who sit in the park and talk are our cultural guardian angels.

4/11/89
SAN ANTONIO

And to start over again, or complete the task, total self-love means you *see* the dance, limbs of trees are dancers in the dawn; truncated, stubby, flat, blossoming tree dancer in the dawn,

I dance in a dream,
am green.
Must die in the cycle and in the fury of
fertility, flap alive, sing my death song
my life song.
In the decay and debris of my days
I have found the old face in me
and the child's face,
brown eyes—
so sensitive when
he wants to be
in the ashes
in the smoke
of blessings.

◆

I am sitting in the poet's backyard.
A green and yellow truck sits in the dug-out sand pit.
An Olmec face rises out of the ground.
Dew evaporates into the sun-rays.
Sunlight breathes its glowing breath into the morning.
Clothesline. Wooden steps grooved with feet going

up and down in and out of the back door.
> (The feel of black wings at dawn
> flapping between railroad cars,
> the iron of the world!)
An old black car seat against the tree
blue plastic k-mart kiddie pool,
a leaning sweat lodge facing east like a scrawny old bony
jaguar prowling in the trees,
> the peg-leg paws of the sweat lodge,
> are my own reaching into the world.
A sidewalk in the middle of the yard
goes straight back to a whitewashed storage shack.
> (Voice speaking in Spanish in the next yard.
> Cat's meow. A bird trills. Another cackles.
> O, the sun, shine on me!)
An old coca-cola machine against the shack.
Two tables for gatherings of guests.

> What kind of sanctuary is this?
> The collected icons of a brother's journey.
A brother who has burned his life
like incense burned to the four directions,
in the silence watched his words spiral up and cloud his soul
> filling the earthen eyes with joy
> and tongue-splashing thirst-fulfilling songs!

He reminds me of red chile, cedar, piñon and those rugged arroyos
whose rocks are God vowels and dew-gleaming verbs,
> when we could speak earth
> and lives were seeds
> planted in our palms to grow green
> futures.
This age is such a nightmare.
To think of the beauty and then the ripping of earth apart.
> We must heal *HER!*
> *WE MUST!*

With our breath
   our bones
      the paltry fabric of our skin, cover HER
      through the cold night of human history.
Our relationships suffer. Earthquakes are chills clacking
with fever, earth is sick—
      we feed her poison
      we close doors
      we turn our backs
      we flee her plea for help
      we sit and drink
      laughing as she dies
      along each roadside!

Forgive me earth, Great Mother Earth, my magic is poor.
   Forgive!

4/12/89
MICHIGAN

    It is time for us to lessen our addictive ties to theorizing
and intellectual posing. Shut the cameras down and fold up
the landscape partitions. We must have poets and writers who
are generous and compassionate, and who convey their love
for the earth, offering us a true gift from the heart.
    We have had enough brilliant mental dazzle, that
ultimately results in a better bomb or ways of doing things
faster. Ideas are glitter-flakes, cerebral lice, when emotions
are ignored. A colonized people must reach to the caves in
the heart and awaken the sleeping primal dragon that has
kept the fire in its encrusted tabernacle of stone.

◆

I spoke last night about how La Raza carries the *mark*—it is a mark of shame that balances our humility and honor to keep us in harmony with the universe.

Every culture has a mark—ours is a spiritual creative shame-mark given us in the intercellular genes, legacy from a dark time when all of our tribe's artifacts, customs, *santos,* religious rites were destroyed.

The mark makes us humble—gives us honor, keeps us in check, in balance. A spiritual shame-mark that ties us to all things vulnerable and balanced.

Where does our pride come from? Once we were a strong formidable tribe, touching the heavens with our thoughts, seeding the earth with our flowers, close to gods and goddesses, breath-close.

But then havoc and destruction, an age of darkness, in which we inherited our trail of tears, in which our children were massacred; in which, despite our helplessness, we inherited *la marca,* and we are marked by the gods, by the great circle of life.

The mark has kept us alive—has gifted us as a people with reverence and measure toward our brothers and sisters.

Great boxers have that quality. They fight with honor and, whether they win or lose, carry *la marca* of shame in the soul that humanizes the war-grounds with human dimensions.

La marca nurtures us—certainly germinates in me a peaceful surrender of spirit that allows for honorable living, that has helped me to survive. It's a survival tool, a blessing of the highest kind.

Jesus had a mark. What empowered Dr. King, a man the KKK threw piss at when he marched for equal rights, to go on to Selma, was that he knew shame, knew it well. He knew the mark people carry in their lives, that make them do such crazy things to conceal it.

It's a springboard to strength to know our *marca*—which each of us carries down the generations as a gift. May we never lose our shame.

You see families killing each other because their shame cannot be endured. The worst that can happen to a family is shame, and hiding it forces them to violence.

Let there be primal shame, spiritual shame, and let us allow our grief and the fragile flowering of love for each other.

◆

THOUGHT

We must think majestically, be cured of our theoretical anemia. We are a people who think in metaphor. It is our way of seeing, our way of giving gifts to each other. We must not be sucked into bloodless, dialectical, theorizing skirmishes. Without metaphor, our thoughts leak away through the holes in the roof of our hypothesis.

We must create passageways among the islands as the Aztecs did, delivering flowers of ideas to each other.

> I am the flower bearer
> in my visitations a boatman
> paddling among the islands
> delivering, uniting them
> with flower-ideas.

◆

In New York, asked by students about my Indian-ness, I said this:

> The Aztecas were a tribe of *indios* who
> saw a sign. (Eagle and snake.)
> I have seen signs, many signs,
> all my life, leading me to take a path,
> a direction, to go forth

in my destiny and fulfill my purpose.
When the Aztecs arrived, they must have
been tired, weary, a ragged band
of desert vermin.
Other tribes must have asked them,
"You say you are *indio,* but
what is your name, where do you come from,
what is your tribe. . . ?"
And they answered—
"The sun, the eagle, the snake
  have spoken to us,
  have led us here to fulfill
  our purpose on earth."

I feel the same.
I don't know where I come from, not really—
it's too far in the past.
But there are signs, clues, messages in the moon,
in the cycles of seasons I see,
in the stones, eagles, trees, in the four directions—
in them is the womb of wind
I howl with,
blowing my whistle,
my ancient song.

They gave me a card of tribal affiliation. I tore it up.
I have a feeling I am very old, very old.
Our tribe suffered terrible destruction,
blood reeks in the memory.
In a dark age we wandered in a chosen field
of power
in the Southwest, it was/is our homeland—
we lived there, prospered,
and then were repeatedly
slaughtered by plunderers
who reduced our numbers

infected us with their sickness.
      Our dead
      filled dark night
      and day
      with empty eyes
      under the sun.
Before memory we were
before rocks
before blossoms could eat wind, growing plump,
eating sun—
      before all of this
      we were.

      Then a white night fell
      our name burned
      our faces were erased.
      We lived on roots, butterflies, snakes,
      watching the eagle carefully
      until it called out to us
      and we came from darkness,
      the creative dark,
      into our own again.

And when we came
everywhere we went, each tribe we met
asked us, "And who are you?"
And we answered, "Your ancestors, your family,
      tribu de Chicanos. . . . "

◆

There is a sadness in the house of poets
in the studios of painters,
and now in my own arms.
I rock it. I am all poets.
There comes a sadness to their yard

like a lost friend,
a brown-skinned stranger
asleep in the elm leaves.
    In the easels and pens
    its hair stiffens blue
    its eyes are sad words
    of things lost
    its features speak pain
    in the journeys
    toward myth, heart
    beats in pigments and words.

Sad yards
sad rooms—
lovers who died too soon.

♦

I want to belong to others.
I want to be part of their lives.
I spent a lifetime
putting on their shoes
fitting on their shirts
sleeping in their homes
clapping to their music
borrowing their tools
walking through their lives—
    I want to belong to them.

♦

Give me a gift
I give you a gift
in just talking
truthfully to each other.

◆

Say a prayer every time
before you start to write a poem—
                    pray.

◆

Art is:
     the first step to vision-making toward healing the wounds,
healing. In the wound is where the red corn grows.

4/17/89
HARVARD

     I raised my shirt in the faculty lounge and showed a friend
the bullet wounds in my body. I told him I had followed
my craft, my vocation as a poet, reverently.

◆

     Hospitality: In every city I visited, I stayed with friends,
usually poets. They are my home, their ideas and feelings make
roots of my feet. And when I stand upon stages to read my
poetry, I feel the roots crack the boards, dig deep under,
go down, plunging into the furious bowels of Mother Earth,
into her,
          where my friends' spirits
          nurture the roots
          and make what I am saying
          the poem I am reading
          flowers I toss
          to the audience, into their laps,
          their hair.

In the ancient role
of Flower-Bearer
I reconnect the islands, as the Aztecs once did,
with passages of flowers.
From Sacramento to New York, Chicago to Albuquerque,
I connect the islands
of people through song.

◆

For all the times
I told my friends
I would call
and did not call,
I would come
and did not come,
I ask your forgiveness.
I graft myself to the moment,
become part of the dream
growing out of us
into a vision, a hope.
Your allowances
to let me become who I wish
is friendship,
your forgiveness
is our gift.
Thank you.
We are counterparts, half-faces
becoming full moons.

◆

LOVE

If you could pulverize
a moon rock,

moon marrow, dream corn-paste
to yellow powder . . .
This morning
you rubbed
powder on my face
and hands
and couldn't remember the name
of the moon
when I asked.
Today I am fragrant with moon powder,
as fruit trees by their fruit in season
I am ripe with your love.

5/21/89
SOUTH SIDE BURQUE

Night. The sounds of the barrio swirl and growl—great
roars come through the neighborhood. Celebrations that high
school has ended. Smokey Robinson pleads and wails to a
full moon. Children splash—swing bats at piñatas—turn three
times blindfolded. The earth, the ditches, the people, twirl
into a rose of experience, thorned memory, soft endurance,
the war of wanting and not having. . . .

6/6/89
SAN ANTONIO

The sun shimmers on the aluminum wing
as we taxi away.
I look forward to winter in New Mexico,
to gathering myself against the cold
and feeling warmth of my body.
                              It is good to be alive

even at 20,000 feet cruising
20 miles from Waco.
70 degrees—still no sign of rain.
Texas cracks from lack of rain
    from lack of respect
    from cash that can't buy rain.

Wouldn't it be great if the pilot read us a poem we passengers could use to contemplate the sky and clouds and our lives?

The stewardesses hack at the dining-cart doors, bang them open and slam them shut. They look like lifeguards or glasses of orange juice. They wear the same black shoes simple village girls wear. I pull the shade down halfway, draw a blanket over my legs, and realize, as I look at the clouds, how much older I am.

6/21/89
SANTA BARBARA

I keep thinking, here in Santa Barbara, as I look at the many sailboats dipping elegantly out to sea, what it would be like to create them in new forms. What if all those yachts

    were *indio* canoes,
    if the clubhouse became a ceremonial dancing ground?
    Only the sea responds to these dreams.
    On each wave a thousand spirits dance
    climbing each terrace of whitecap foam
    drumbeating at the shores
    of my dream.

♦

Birds know when the grapes are ripe.

Glossary of Spanish Terms

alabado: religious hymn of praise to God, the Virgin, or the saints. In its New Mexican form it may utilize both Spanish and Tewa (Amerindian language) words. It is typically characterized by rhythms similar to those of Gregorian chant and/or Amerindian chants.

arroyo: stream or gully formed by heavy rains

Aztlán: Aztec mythological "land to the north," believed to refer to the southwestern United States

caldo: soup

las calles: the streets

camarada: comrade; friend, buddy

canción: song

cantina: bar, tavern

carnalismo: consanguinity; brotherhood

Chicanismo: social and political awareness and ethnic spirit typifying the Chicano Movement

chuco: shortening of *pachuco;* Chicano zoot suiter

corazón: literally, heart; more broadly, deep feeling, compassion

gavacho: Anglo-American; *gringo*

la gente: the Chicano people

indio: American Indian

llano: plains (geographical feature)

malías: sick; strung out on drugs

menudo: Mexican-style tripe stew

mestizaje: the mixing of Spanish and Amerindian blood

mestizo: a person of mixed Spanish and Amerindian heritage

pachuco: Chicano zoot suiter

piñon: (plural, *piñones*) pine nut

primo: cousin

la raza: literally, the race; specifically used to indicate Chicanos

resolana: a gathering for the purpose of exchanging barrio news

santo: saint; also can refer to the image of a saint in religious paintings

salsa: spicy condiment; also music with a Latin-American beat

vato: guy, dude

viga: wooden ceiling beam; in New Mexican architecture, typically an exposed log beam

About the Author

Jimmy Santiago Baca was born in Santa Fe and grew up on the plains near the Manzano Mountains of New Mexico. His publications include the following collections of poetry, published by New Directions: *IMMIGRANTS IN OUR OWN LAND* (1979, reprinted in 1991), *BLACK MESA POEMS* (1989), and *MARTÍN & MEDITATIONS ON THE SOUTH VALLEY* (1987), for which he won the 1988 American Book Award.

Additional awards he has received are: the National Endowment for the Arts Creative Writing Fellowship for Poetry (1987); the Vogelstein Foundation Award (1988); the Wallace Stevens Fellowship, Yale University (1989); the Hispanic Heritage Award for Literature (1989); the Regents' Lecturer Award, University of California, Berkeley (1989); and the Pushcart Prize (1989).

Mr. Baca has been a lecturer and writer in residence at Santa Monica College, California. He has given poetry readings and led poetry workshops in colleges, universities, prisons, and community centers throughout the United States and in Mexico. Baca is in a motion picture slated to be released in 1992 by Hollywood Pictures.

Jimmy Baca lives on a small farm outside of Albuquerque, New Mexico, with his wife Beatrice and his sons Antonio and Gabriel.